GENESIS

IN

THE LIGHT OF THE NEW TESTAMENT.

By F. W. Grant.

WIPF & STOCK · Eugene, Oregon

Wipf and Stock Publishers
199 W 8th Ave, Suite 3
Eugene, OR 97401

Genesis in the Light of the New Testament
By Grant, F. W.
Softcover ISBN-13: 978-1-7252-7565-2
            ISBN-13: 978-1-7252-7566-9
Publication date 3/30/2020
Previously published by Loizeaux Brothers, 1900

CONTENTS.

Page.

PART I.—God's Counsels in Creation.

Introductory................................... 5
The Individual Application..................... 11
The Dispensational Application 23
Paradise 33

PART II.—Divine Life in its Various Aspects.

1. Adam....................................... 37
2. The Carnal and Spiritual Seed............... 53
3. Noah....................................... 65
4. Abraham 78
    Lot...................................... 116
    The Philistines.......................... 125
5. Isaac. { The Dispensational Application...... 134
          { The Individual   "   143
6. Jacob. { The Dispensational   "   154
          { The Individual   "   161
7. Joseph. { The Dispensational   "   173
           { The Individual   "   185

GENESIS

IN

THE LIGHT OF THE NEW TESTAMENT.

PART I.

GOD'S COUNSELS IN CREATION. (Chap. i. & ii.)

Introductory.

IN seeking to develop (as is now my purpose) the
truths of the *New* Testament from the history
of the Old, it is the typical meaning with which
we have to do. The divine glory, as seen in
Moses' face, was vailed to the people addressed;
for us, the vail is done away in Christ. The words
of the apostle with reference to Israel's history, it
can scarcely be doubted, apply no less to that
which was but prefatory to theirs,—"Now, all
these things happened unto them for ensamples
[*lit*. types]; and are written for our admonition,
upon whom the ends of the world are come."

He gives us, moreover, many of the details,—
Adam, a type of Christ; Eve, of the Church;
Abel's offering, of the sinner's acceptance; Noah's
salvation by the ark, of our own in Christ; Mel-
chizedek, king of righteousness and peace; the
story of Abraham's two sons; and a *hint*, at least,
as to the offering up of Isaac (Gal. iii. 16, 17.). Nor
is this all that is commonly recognized as typical,
though some no doubt would have us stop where

the inspired explanation stops. But in that case, how large a part of what is plainly symbolical would be lost to us!—the larger part of the Levitical ordinances, not a few of the parables of the Lord Himself, and almost the whole of the book of Revelation. Surely none could deliberately accept a principle which would lock up from us so large a part of the inspired Word.

Still many have the thought that it would be safer to refrain from typical applications of the historical portions where no inspired statement authenticates them as types at all. Take, however, such a history as that of Joseph, which no direct scripture speaks of as a type, yet the common consent of almost all receives as such; or Isaac's sacrifice, of the significance of which we have the merest hint. The more we consider it, the more we find it impossible to stop short here. Fancy, no doubt, is to be dreaded. Sobriety and reverent caution are abundantly needful. But so are they every where. If we profess wisdom, we become fools: subjection to the blessed Spirit of God, and to the Word inspired of Him, are our only safeguards here and elsewhere.

When we look a little closer, we find that the types are not scattered by hap-hazard in the Old-Testament books. On the contrary, they are connected together and arranged in an order and with a symmetry which bear witness to the divine hand which has been at work throughout. We find Exodus thus to be the book of redemption; Leviticus, to speak of what suits God with us in the sanctuary,—of sanctification; then Numbers, to give the wilderness-history—our walk with God (*after* redemption and being brought to Him where He is,) through the world. Each individual type in these different books will be found to have most intimate and significant relation to the great central thought pervading the book. This, when laid hold of, confirms immensely our apprehension of the general and particular meaning, and gives it a force little if at all short of absolute demonstration.

The great central truth in Genesis is "LIFE." It thus begins where all begins actually for the soul. God is seen in it as Life-giver, Creator; this involving necessarily also that He is sovereign in purpose and Almighty* in execution. This is why Genesis is, as it has been called, "the seed-plot of the Bible," because it is the book of the counsels of the sovereign and almighty God.

But "life" is, so to speak, the key-note—the thread upon which all else is strung. Genesis is plainly almost entirely a series of biographies. It divides, after the introductory account of creation, in chapters i. and ii, into *seven* of these, in which we have a perfect picture of divine life in the soul, from its almost imperceptible beginning to its full maturity.

Adam gives us the beginning, when, with the entrance of God's Word, light comes into the soul of a sinner, and God meets him *as* such with the provision of His grace. (Chap. iii.)

Then, (Chap. iv. and v.) we have the history of the two "seeds," and their antagonism,—a story which has its counterpart in the history of the world at large, but also in every individual soul

---

*Which is plainly God's revelation of Himself to Abraham, Isaac, and Jacob, as distinct from Jehovah to Israel (see Exod. vi. 3). In the rest of the Pentateuch the word occurs only in Balaam's prophecy (Num. xxiv.), and only in Ruth besides of all the historical books.

where God has wrought, and where the "flesh lusteth against the Spirit, and the Spirit against the flesh, and these are contrary the one to the other."

Next, Noah's passage through the judgment of the old world into a new scene, accepted of God in the sweet savor of sacrifice, is the type of where salvation puts us—"in Christ, a new creation: old things passed away, and all things become new." (Chap. vi.–xi. 9.)

Abraham's Canaan-life—pilgrim and stranger, but a worshiper, gives us the fruit and consequence of this—a "*walk* in Him" whom we have received. (Chap. xi. 10–xxi.)

Then, Isaac, our type as "sons," (Gal. iv. 28.) speaks to us of a self-surrender into a Father's hands, the door into a life of quiet and enjoyment, as it surely is. (Chap. xxii.–xxiv. 33.)

Jacob speaks of the *discipline* of sons, by which the crooked and deceitful man becomes Israel, a prince with God,—a chastening of love, dealing with the fruits of the *old* nature in us. (Chap. xxvi. 34–xxxvii. 1.)

While Joseph, the fullest image of Christ, suffers, not for *sin*, but for *righteousness'* sake, and attains supremacy over the world, and fullness of blessing from the almighty One, his strength. (Chap. xxxvii. 2–l.)

All this we may more fully see hereafter. Even this hint of it may make plain what I have already stated to be the main feature of the book, with which the first section corresponds in the closest way. Like many another first section, but perhaps beyond any other, it is really a sort of table of contents to the rest of the book. It is of course much more than that, as we shall see, if the Lord give wisdom to unfold what this story of creation gives us.

It is, as all else here, a type, while it is none the less on that account a literal history. Its spiritual meaning in no wise turns it into myth or fable, as some would assume. "All these things happened unto them," says the apostle,—so the things *really* happened, but—"for types." What importance must attach, then, to a "type," to produce which God has actually modeled the history of the world from the beginning! With what reverence should we listen to the utterances so strangely given, so marvelously "written for our admonition"! Instead of setting aside the literal record of creation, it surely confirms it in the highest degree that the Creator should demonstrate Himself the new Creator, and show how in laying the foundations of the earth which sin has cursed and death has scarred, He who seeth the end from the beginning had even then before Him, in the depths and counsels of His heart, a scene into which, secure in its unchanging Head, sin and death no more should enter—which they should nevermore defile! It is divine, this record: true, of course, then, and infinitely more,—although faith be needed for the realization of it.

I do not doubt that the story before us is not merely even a single, but a twofold type; finding its fulfillment in two spheres, which are very generally correspondent to one another. The world without has its reflection in the world within us. So the steps in the divine dealing with the world at large have their correspondence with His dealing with us as individuals. In our consideration

of them, this individual application will come first.
It is that which is most prominent all through, and
which links the whole series of types together;
and this has its significance for us. In men's
thoughts you will find, as what they imagine to be
advanced and liberal views, the progress of the *race*
putting out of sight the interest of the individual:
they speak much of *man*, think little of *men.** It
is not so with God; the blessing of the race is
reached (with Him) through the blessing of the
individual, and not one is overlooked. Nay, "not
a sparrow falls to the ground without your Father." This is what is in His heart, whatever the
perplexity which sin has introduced; and oh how
profoundly needful for us the assurance of this!
It may do for philosophy to proclaim the grandeur
of general laws, to which the individual good must
give place; but the grip of this iron machinery
has none of the comfort of the grasp of a Father's
hand. The *heart of God* alone suffices the hearts
which He has made.

Let us take, then, this individual application
first, and let creation preach to us lessons which
may be happily familiar to us, and yet have a new
charm as preached thus, where (as all preaching
should be,) the sermon is an anthem, and the anthem is in the many voices of the universe—the
revelation-chorus to which all will come at last:
"And every creature which is in heaven, and on
the earth, and under the earth, and such as are in
the sea, and all that are in them, heard I saying,
'Blessing and honor and glory and power be unto
Him that sitteth upon the throne, and unto the
Lamb forever and ever!'"

*As, *e.g.*, Dr. Temple's "Education of the World," in "Essays and Reviews."

The Individual Application.

THERE are two smaller sections of the first natural division of the book of Genesis. The first (chap. i.–ii. 3.) gives us the work of God and His rest; the second, (chap. ii. 4–25.) *God in relationship* with the creature He has made. Hence, in this latter part the covenant-name is for the first time introduced; it is not "God" merely, but "*The Lord God*"—Jehovah. We shall see more fully the force of this hereafter. In this double account there is an exquisite beauty, which the unbelief that cavils at it can never see.

It is necessary also to distinguish from the six days' work, what has been strangely confounded with it, the primitive creation of the first chapter and verse, and the ruin into which it had fallen when "without form and void, and darkness on the face of the deep." This used to be, and I suppose still may be called, the common view; and yet the more one looks at the passage the more it seems impossible to make such a mistake. For plainly the work of the six days begins with this: "God said, 'Let there be light;' and there was light." But as plainly the earth, although waste and desolate, was there before that, not created then. Moreover the words "without form and void," for which "waste and desolate" would be preferable as a reading, imply distinctly a state of ruin, and not of development; while a passage in which the first of these terms is used asserts expressly that the Lord did not create the earth so.*

Nor can it be said that the exigencies of a geo-

*It is the word rendered "in vain," Isaiah xiv. 18. The two are found together in Isaiah xxxiv. 11 and Jeremiah iv. 23.

logical difficulty have forced such a construction of the opening words of this account. Augustine, who knew nothing of such a difficulty, long ago decided for it from the mere force of the language used. The requirement of it by the mere typical view I am just now advocating, is independent of it also, and yet quite as urgent; for it makes the six days' work a remoulding of a former lapsed creation, the *new* birth, as we may call it, of a world. How plainly significant is that, at once! And such a view of it the words themselves necessitate.

There was, then, a primary creation, afterward a fall; first, "heaven and earth," in due order; then earth without a heaven—in darkness, and buried under "a deep" of salt and barren and restless waters. What a picture of man's condition, as fallen away from God! How complete the confusion! how profound the darkness! how deep the restless waves of passion roll over the wreck of what was once so fair! "The wicked are like the troubled sea, when it cannot rest, whose waters cast up mire and dirt."

Then mark how the new birth begins: "The Spirit of God moved [or *brooded*] upon the face of the waters. And God said, 'Let there be light.'" From the Spirit and the Word it comes: we are "born of the Spirit;" we are "born of the incorruptible seed" of "the Word of God." And "the entrance of Thy Word giveth *light*." How faithfully this beginning of creative work depicts that more mighty still in the human soul, and assures of what was even then for us in the counsels of divine wisdom! Truly His "delights were with the sons of men."

The first day gives us, then, the entrance of the Word giving light. The state of the creature is manifested by it, but as yet it shines on naught but desolation. Nothing is changed, save the dark-ness; there is nothing that God can find of good but the light itself. *That* He pronounces so— severs it from the darkness and gives it a place and a name; but the darkness too is named, and has its place, and is not all removed. For not in the earth itself is the source of light, and when turned away from this it is still dark. Practically, the day is not all light, but "evening and morning" make it up; yet, though darkness is in itself "night," it is well to note that it is never, now that light has once come in, simple and absolute night any more, but "evening;" some rays of the day there ever are; and in God's order, too, an evening surely giving place to morning. And then again, as to the "morning," its promise of the perfect "day" is never realized until God's work is wrought out and His Sabbath is reached; then, indeed, there is no more evening, or morning either, but "day," without mixture or decline— God's great finality—is fully come.

I do not believe this needs interpreting; the significance of its voice is not hard to apprehend. And thus not only "day unto day uttereth speech," but also "night unto night showeth knowledge." Dear reader, if perchance one there be who may read this, down into whose desolate soul the light has shone, revealing not good but ill, when good has begun to have attraction too, but there is none —you are learning but this first day's lesson. Spite of all that is disclosed, the light is good. Welcome it as from God, the beginning of His gracious work in you, the promise of the day that yet shall come.

The second stage of this divine work is the making of the "firmament," or "expanse," by which a separation of the waters is effected. Strangely misunderstood as it has been by some, it is, one would think, self-evidently, the formation of the atmospheric "heavens," which draw up now (as they have been doing ever since) out of the deep below, waters which, purged of their saltness, become the still inexplicably balanced clouds.

The spiritual stage it represents is scarcely more difficult to follow. A separation is now effected, not in the external condition merely, but more inwardly. The unseen things operate upon the soul, and attract affections and desires upward to them. That which was "lust" and "corruption" in a heart away from God is thus purified by the new object. It is the "*kingdom of heaven*" spiritually begun. The heart is under divine government. And while the general state of the creature remains apparently the same (there is still no fruit nor solid ground)— while still "in me, that is, in my flesh, dwells no good thing," yea, while "how to perform that which is good I find not"—still we can say, "To will is present with me," and "with the mind I myself serve the law of God." Peace is not come, nor liberty, nor power; but the heart drawn up to God, that intercourse with heaven is begun which at a further stage shall bring down showers of blessing to fertilize and bring forth fruit to God.

Still, by the Word is every stage produced. Each time God speaks. It is not mere development of what lies unfolded in the earliest germ. Step by step the forthputting of divine power accomplishes counsels that are all divine. "We are His workmanship"—the patient, perfect elabora-tion of the wisdom of God—"created in Christ Jesus." Happy we, proportionately as we are yielded into His hands, and cast into the mould of His efficacious Word!

The "third day" speaks to the Christian heart of resurrection. It is marked here by resurrection-power: the earth comes up out of the waters. That which can be wrought upon and made fruitful is now brought up from under the irreclaimable waste of sea. This is not removed, but bounded and restrained; it cannot return to cover the earth. Its existence is indeed distinctly recognized; it gets for the first time its name from God; in the *new* earth there will be none. (Rev. xxi. 1.) Meanwhile He lays the foundations of the earth,* that it never should be moved at any time.

This is only the first half of the third day. It is a *double* day, as we may say, with God. Twice He speaks; twice He pronounces His work good. In the first half, the earth is separated from the waters; in the second, it brings forth the "grass," the "herb," and "the fruit-tree yielding fruit." Let us examine the spiritual meaning of all this.

"Risen with Christ" is the truth which inevita-bly connects itself with such a figure. Christ hav-ing died and risen again for us, His resurrection no less than His death is ours. His death is our passage out of our old state and condition as sin-ners—as children of Adam. His resurrection is our entrance into a new state and sphere. "In Christ"—"if any man be" *there*, "he is a new

---

*Not the *world*, but that "dry land" which He has just named "Earth."

creature: old things are passed away; behold, all things are become new."

The attempt to read this by experience has been the loss (practically) of its blessedness. Unable to look within and say *"all* things are new," men have been reduced either to modify this as if it were too extreme a statement, or else to doubt if they were really Christians. Moreover, the trying to produce such a state of things within them has resulted in constant disappointment and real loss of power. They have sought to mend self and produce there what they might find satisfaction in, instead of turning away from self altogether, to find in occupation with Christ and with His love true power over it.

But it is not "if any man be born again" or "be converted." It is not the result of the work within us that is stated, but the result of the new position before God in which we stand. Acceptance *in* Christ is acceptance *as* Christ. It is no question, therefore, of what is in *us* at all, but of what is in Christ for us; thus viewed, old things are indeed passed away, and all things become new.

Christ's resurrection has put us in this new place; we are risen with Him. The acceptance of this blessed fact brings us into rest and peace, and sets us on vantage-ground above the water-floods. It is for us spiritually God's bringing up the earth from under the waves, and settling it upon its everlasting foundations. True, the waters are not removed, the flesh is not become spirit, nor done away; on the contrary, it is now for the first time fully recognized as there, and incurable—has its place and its name defined; but the man in Christ has risen out of it—is "not in the flesh." It is in him; but he is not *it*, nor *in* it.

This is the first part of the day of resurrection only. The second part gives us the fruitfulness which is the immediate consequence of this; for being now "made free from sin," we are "become the servants of righteousness." Notice some features here.

God calls the dry land "Earth." In the original, this word is derived from one which means "crumbling,"* and it is manifestly a chief condition of fertility that earth *should* crumble. The more continually its clods break up into ever finer dust, the more its promise to the husbandman; and this is a simple lesson and a great one. The brokenness of spirit which makes no resistance to the Father's hand is a main element of fertility in souls wherein He works. It is not power He seeks from us, but weakness; not resistant force, but "yieldingness" to Him. All power is His: His strength is perfected in weakness.

The character depicted here is beautifully illustrated in this very "third day" state in Romans viii. Up to the very end of chapter vii, in the well-known experience already alluded to, the man in question is profoundly conscious of two "I's" in opposition to each other; "with the mind I myself serve the law of God, but with the flesh the law of sin." There is the struggle that convulses him; one part for God and good, the other always contrary—alas! always the stronger too. "The law of the Spirit of life in Christ Jesus" delivers him "from the law of sin and death." Then there are two contrary parties still. But there is a change.

---

*'*Erets* from *Ratz*, according to Parkhurst, Heb. Lex.

The flesh is there indeed yet, and nowise altered, but its now victorious antagonist is not "I myself." That is sunk; it is now "flesh" and "Spirit" that conflict—the Holy Ghost in place of "me."

Oh for constant realization of this! the dropping (not of the flesh—that cannot be here, but) of that good and right-minded and holy "I" which is ever weakness, ever inability, with all its pious resolution and good will! "I live—*not* I—but Christ liveth in me."

Even thus is the fertile earth produced. Out of weakness, out of nothingness, out of infirmities, which make the power of Christ to rest upon us, and leave us clay in the potter's hands. The more we know the reality of resurrection, the more shall we know of this.

Then as to the fruit. **There** is progress; from grass and herb to "fruit-tree yielding fruit, whose seed is in itself upon the earth"—another beautiful figure that. The fruit bears within itself the capacity of self-perpetuation. Itself for the Master's use (and it is well to remember that), the seed is in this fruit according to its kind,—love to produce love, and so on. If we want to find love, we must *show* it. And the riper the fruit is for the Master's taste, the riper the seed is also; the best ripe fruit is that which has hung in the sun most.

All this is simple; and it shows there is a real voice in creation round, to be understood if we have will to understand. The works of His hand bear witness to Himself,—creation to redemption —things seen to the unseen; the thoughts of God's heart, the depths of His love. It is not a mere *accommodation* of these things we are making; they are *designed* witness, though Christ must be the key to all.

And now we are come to the fourth day. Here the entire scene is changed. It is not the laying the foundations of the earth any more, but the garnishing of the heavens. Sun and moon are ordained as light-givers to the earth now made, and for signs and for seasons, for days and years.

And we are not only "risen with Christ," but in Christ, heavenly; "seated together in heavenly places in Christ Jesus." This truth necessarily follows that of resurrection, and no view of our new creation could be in any wise complete which left out this. Here it follows, then, in very natural order, and the language of the type is not hard to apprehend. "Heaven" is, I doubt not, its own symbol, as indeed the firmament, the lower heaven, gives its name to the unseen and spiritual heaven, God's dwelling-place. Applying it in this way, the first object seen in it speaks for itself. Scrip. ture too applies it (Mal. iv. 2.). The great luminary of the day, the source of heat and light to the earth, its light self-derived, unchanging, constant as the day it brings,—clearly enough presents to us the "Heavenly One" back in the glory whence He came. The secondary light, light of the night, a light derived from His, yet oh how cold and dull comparatively at the best, changeful—full-faced or dwindled according as it fully faces or is turned away from Him; how easily we read that too, as we read such words as the apostle's here!—"We all, with open face beholding the glory of the Lord, are changed into the same image from glory to glory, even as by the Spirit of the Lord."

Let us learn the lessons that the moon teaches, for they are serious and yet helpful ones. What more serious lesson than her changefulness? She belongs always to heaven according to God's ordinance. Practically, you cannot always find her there; nay, she is more often (to man's sight, of of course,) out of the sky than in it. Then, when there, how seldom full-orbed! how often turned away from him from whom all her radiance comes! For so it does come; her part is reception merely; she shines perforce when in his light, not by her own effort in the least. And could you go up, attracted by her brightness, to see how fair and glorious she was, you would find yourself *there* not in the glory of the moon at all, but of that sun which was bathing her with brightness.

Then notice her from this earth new risen from the waters. Fair she may be, and "precious fruits be brought forth" by her; yea, "abundance of peace as long as the moon endureth;" still the direct sun-rays are another thing, and are the real fructifying, life-giving influence after all. It is one thing to be occupied even with what we are in Christ—and it is our guide in the night, too (Gal. vi. 15, 16.)—it is yet another to be in the glory of His presence, where moon and stars are hidden in the day.

There is much more here, but I leave it and pass on. The fifth day brings another change of scene; and here, when we might have thought that we had left them finally behind, we are brought back again to the barren waste of waters. But now even here the power of God is working; the waters swarm with swarms of living creatures,

and birds fly in the open firmament of heaven. It is still progress in the great creative plan, and new and higher forms of life are reached than heretofore. It is not now grass and herb, but the "living soul," and God blesses them, and bids them multiply.

Can we give this expression? I believe so. There are harmonies elsewhere that will guide us to an understanding of it.

Take one in the order of the Pentateuch itself, where the same thing occurs—a real progress by apparent retrogression. For if Genesis begins (as we have seen it does) with "life," Exodus gives us, very plainly, the *redemption* of God's people; while Leviticus leads us into the sanctuary of God, to learn in His presence what suits Him to whom we are brought and whose we are. Thus all is progress; but at the next step this seems ended, for in Numbers we pass out once more into the world to face the trials of the wilderness and the still worse exposure of ourselves that meets us there.

This seems retrogression; still it is progress after all. There is no dislocation of His plan who is ever working onward to perfection. For the world is surely the place where, after we have known redemption, and the God that has redeemed us too, we are left to be practiced in what we know, that we may be "those who by reason of use, have their senses exercised to discern both good and evil."

There is *discipline* in this; and failure comes out plentifully too; still we are chastened to be partakers of His holiness; the new life in us gets practical form and embodiment, as we may say; in other words—the words of our type—the "living soul" is produced out of the midst of the waters.

For the waters are, as we have seen, the restless and fallen nature of man; and it is this (whether within or without) that makes the wilderness the place of trial that it is; yet out of this evil, divine sovereignty produces good. And again, the "living soul"—since the soul is the seat of desires, appetites, affections, etc.,—may fitly depict the living energies which lay hold of eternal things amid the pressure on every side of what is seen and temporal.*

This, I believe, is the fifth-day scene. One day alone remains, and God's work is complete.

And this day, which is a second "third," has its two parts likewise, as the third day had. First, the *earth* (and not the waters now) bring forth the "living soul." It is not now the fruit of discipline, or the chafing and contact of sin and evil, but the development of what is proper to the new man apart from this. Jacob's and Joseph's lives show us this contrast fully, as we may see more afterward. And like Joseph's too, this sixth day shows us next the rule of the man, God's image. I can but little interpret here, it is true, but the outline is not the less plain because of the meagreness of the interpretation. The mere indication may attract some to look deeper into this final mystery of creative wisdom.

For what remains is rest, and only rest, God's rest in love over His accomplished work. Seven times He has pronounced all "good," the last time "very good." Now "evening" and "morning" come no more, but full, ripe, unending "day"—

---

*Take Philippians iii. as the vivid portrayal of this.

a day blessed and sanctified of God as the day of His rest.

The fuller exposition of this, however, will come more in its place after we have glanced at the dispensational application of the six days' work. For they have their fulfillment also, as I have already said, in the sphere of the world at large, in the progressive steps by which from the beginning divine power and wisdom have been moving on to the accomplishment of that of which eternity alone can fully tell.

The Dispensational Application.

THE ordinary dispensational application of the week of creation is one which has so many adherents, and has given rise to so much speculation otherwise, that we shall do well to look at it before proceeding further. In the words of a modern writer, "In this application, 'one day is as a thousand years.' Six thousand years of labor precede the world's Sabbath. The parallel here has been often traced." It is as old, indeed, as the so-called "Epistle of Barnabas,"* and its scriptural support is supposed to be the passage in 2 Peter iii, already referred to. According to it, the millennial kingdom answers, as the seventh thousand years, to the "seventh day," earth's Sabbath-rest.

---

*Which, it is almost needless to say, was not the production of the scriptural Barnabas, although by the very general voice of antiquity attributed to him. Its date is supposed to be somewhat before the middle of the second century A. D. I quote the passage from the translation in the "Ante-Nicene Christian Library:"—

"Attend, my children, to the meaning of this expression: 'He finished in six days.' This implieth that the Lord will finish all things in six thousand years, for a day is with Him a thousand years. And He Himself testifieth, 'Behold, to-day will be as a thousand years.'" The last is probably an incorrect citation of psalm xc. 4.

But as to the principle, the passage in Peter is no proof at all. It is no statement of time, but the contrary—the simple assurance of how little God counts time as man counts it. It might be as fairly argued from it that the millennial "thousand years" was but a day, as that the creation "days" represented each a thousand years; for it is not only "One day is with the Lord as a thousand years," but also "a thousand years as one day."

Nor is the millennium, with all its blessedness, a proper Sabbath. The apostle represents the "rest" (literally, "Sabbath-keeping,") that remains to the people of God, as *God's* rest, and that surely is, as both the epistle to the Hebrews (chap. iv. 9, 10.) and the book of Genesis show, His *ceasing* from His work. But in the millennium there is not as yet this. It is the last work-day rather, and not till the new heavens and earth will God's rest be come. The seventh day is not, then, the type of a millennium at all, but of final and eternal rest.

Moreover, the millennial kingdom answers so fully to the sixth-day rule of the man and woman over the earth, that it is strange how it could escape the notice of those who were seeking a dispensational application of the creation-work. While on the other hand a mere arithmetical interpretation of the days as each a thousand years of the world's history, seems almost self-evidently artificial and unspiritual.

I may leave this, then, to point out what I have no doubt is the real dispensational application. In this it will be found we have but the former interpretation extended and adapted to the larger sphere.

Thus we have here alike a primitive creation

and a fall, and then, too, that work of the Spirit and the Word by which every step toward the blessedness that shall be has been successively produced. The first day has very plainly the features of the age before the flood, when through the word of promise the light shone, but without further interference with the state of the creature. The light fell only upon a ruin. Lust and violence were the general features of man's condition, and furnish a history over which the Spirit of God passes with significant brevity, and which "the troubled sea, when it cannot rest," sufficiently depicts. Upon this world a literal flood passed, and it perished.

The second day gives us the formation of the "heavens," a symbol not hard to read, when we have learnt elsewhere the constant use of these as the seat of authority and power. It is the uniform language of Scripture that "the heavens rule." The "*sun* to rule by day" is indeed not yet come, nor the moon by night. Naught fills these heavens as yet but "waters"—waters above as well as beneath—the very type of instability. And this makes it the perfect type of what took place when, after the flood, man was put in the place of responsibility to be his brother's keeper. "Whoso sheddeth man's blood, *by man* shall his blood be shed," is the principle, and was the institution, as is plain, of human government. It was the formation of a political "heavens" with, as yet, nothing but waters filling them. And how quickly Noah, the acknowledged head of the new world, drunk with the fruit of his vineyard, exemplified the instability of the type! And from henceforth what has it been but the constant display of this—the want of self-government in those who govern? A step toward the full attainment of God's perfect counsel for the earth it is; even now, power ordained of God, and His ministry for good, and yet a Nero or Caligula may be this "power." And significant it seems that on this second day there is no voice of God pronouncing "good" what is nevertheless for good. Providentially, He may be working blessing by that which in itself He cannot bless. And this is of solemn import for all times and spheres.

The third day following sees the dry land separated from the waters. These waters we have all along seen to be the type of human passion and self-will—what man left to himself exhibits. But this is evidently, on the larger scale we are now taking, just the Gentiles,* and the earth raised up out of these waters is the seed of Abraham after the flesh—that people plowed up with the plowshare of God's holy law, and among whom was sown the seed of the divine Word. Little fruit may it yet have yielded, and given up it may be for its fruitlessness and unprofitableness at the present time; yet it lies but fallow, like the actual land of Israel, waiting for the latter rain and the foretold fertility under the care of the divine husbandry. Nor has the past been only failure. For long the only fruit for God we know was to be found there, and in a sense, of its fruit are even we: "salvation" was "of the Jews." Thus there need be no difficulty in this fertile earth separated from the waters representing Israel's separation

---

*Compare Revelation xvii. 15,—"The waters . . . are peoples and multitudes and nations and tongues."

to God out of all the nations of the world.*

The fourth day's lesson is one simpler still. The lights set in the heavens speak very plainly of Christ and of the Church; or, as we are accustomed to say, of the Christian dispensation. The mystery here we have already glanced at, for the individual application scarcely differs from the dispensational. Here Christ, revealed by the Holy Ghost, shines out for men in the word of His grace; while the Church is the responsible reflector of Christ, His epistle to the world. The word of the Spirit to the churches (Rev. ii, iii.) may give us the moon's phases in the night of Christ's absence — that night surely now fast drawing to a close.

Let this scene preach to us that all true and divine light now is heavenly. To let our "light shine" is naught else than to let men see we belong to another sphere, are not of the world even as Christ was not; and to let them see our faces brightened with the joy of what He is, our hearts *satisfied* with Himself, and so independent of the broken cisterns from which they strive to draw refreshment. This was once actually the Church's testimony, in those days when men were "turned to God from idols . . . to wait for His Son from heaven." Alas! while the Bridegroom tarried, the light grew dim. "They all slumbered and slept." The only light for the world is still the virgin's lamp as she goes forth to meet the Bridegroom.

His call of them to Himself will close this dis-

*To those acquainted with the meaning of Revelation xiii, it will not be insignificant that the last Gentile empire should be figured there in the beast *from the sea*, the Jewish Antichrist in the second beast *from the earth.*

pensation, and then will dawn that strange and solemn fifth day, when once again the "waters" will have risen and covered every thing; the time of which the ninety-third psalm speaks, though as of a past condition,—"The floods have lifted up, O Lord, the floods have lifted up their voice; the floods lift up their waves;" but only to prove that "the Lord on high is mightier than the noise of many waters, yea, than the mighty waves of the sea."

The time of the world's discipline will have come, "the hour of trial upon all the world, to try them that dwell upon the earth." These waters speak of a universal *Gentile* (that is, lawless) state; of the working of man's wild will: "upon the earth distress of nations, with perplexity; *the sea and the waves roaring;* men's hearts failing them for fear, and for looking after those things which are coming on the earth."

But when God's "judgments are upon the earth, the inhabitants of the world will learn righteousness." This is the secret of the waters producing the living creature. It is the time when (the heavenly people being gathered home) God will be preparing a people for earthly blessing. Brief may be the time in which He does this: Scripture is none the less full of the detail of the mighty work to be done. And a most real and necessary step it will be toward that reign of righteousness and peace which the sixth day so plainly figures.

For here the rule of the man in God's image and likeness can scarcely fail to make itself understood by those who look for the Lord then to take a throne which as Son of Man He can call His own

(Rev. i. 13; iii. 21.), and which therefore He can share with His people, as He cannot share His Father's throne. The first Adam, we are told by the apostle (Rom. v. 14.), was the image of the One to come; even as he also tells us (Eph. v. 25, 32.) Eve is of that Church which He will present to Himself without spot or blemish. Thus we can scarcely by any possibility mistake the spiritual meaning of the sixth day's work.

In that day, too, the *earth* brings forth the living creature. "*Israel* shall bud and blossom, and fill the face of the earth with fruit." She shall be Jezreel, "the seed of God," and "I will sow her to Me in the earth," says the Lord God.

And as this is the last work-day, not yet Sabbath rest, so is the millennial kingdom in the hands of Him who takes it to bring all things back to God. "He must reign till He hath put all enemies under His feet. And when all things shall be subdued under Him, then shall the Son also Himself be subject unto Him that put all things under Him, that GOD may be all in all." Then, and not till then, is the Sabbath reached.

"And on the seventh day God had ended His work which He had made; and He rested on the seventh day from all His work which He had made. And God blessed the seventh day, and sanctified it, because that in it He had rested from all His work which God created and made."

Here God alone appears, and the work being ended, all being according to His mind, He sanctifies the day of His rest. How significant this of the day, never to give place to another, when redemption being fully accomplished, and all things brought to the pattern proposed in the eternal

counsels, He shall indeed put the seal of His perfect delight upon the whole new creation, hallowed
to Himself forever! How could God rest short of
this consummation? Then indeed He will be
"all," and that be the simple, full expression of
the creature's blessedness, and of its perpetuity
as well.

Some details of this final blessing are presented
to us in the following section, which concludes
this first part of Genesis (chap. ii. 4–25.); but before we go on to this let us only for a moment compare the meaning of the lives which shortly follow
in the book—a meaning already briefly glanced at
—with that now given of these six creative days.
We shall find in them, not absolute identity (for
Scripture never merely repeats itself), but a
parallel of a most striking sort; a remarkable
witness of the internal unity of Scripture, and of
this first book. How easy to understand that
Genesis is, as it has been called, the "seed-plot of
the Bible," when it is thus in the whole the expansion of those divine counsels which have their indication already in the creative work itself! And
so indeed it is.

But it is plain that here the *seven* lives recorded
in Genesis must have their counterparts in the *six*
days' work; there is none to the seventh-day rest.
And it is as plain that the last life, Joseph, the most
perfect type of Christ, the man, God's image, answers here precisely to the sixth, and not to the
seventh day. We shall obtain a seventh day then,
so to speak, by taking the third day as a double
one. We have already noticed that it is so, for
God speaks twice, and twice pronounces His work

good. Looking at the days thus, let us compare the double series.*

Now, beginning with the third chapter, the story of Adam is just the exposure of man, such as the fall has made him: the light let in upon his condition, with no apparent internal change. And this is the truth of the first day.

Next, as to the division of the waters on the second day, we have already seen that its lesson corresponds with that of the two seeds into which the human race at once divides: the opposition, namely, between the carnal and spiritual mind, which every renewed soul is conscious of.

Then, if the third day give us in the earth's coming up out of the waters the type of how we too rise up out of the inundation of sin into the place at once of rest and power over it, the third life, Noah's, gives us as plainly our passage in Christ our ark out of the scene of the sin and judgment of man in the flesh to that in which blessing is secured by the sweet savor of accepted sacrifice.

The *fruit* of the second half of the third day, again, is seen in Abraham, the practical life of faith which follows upon this.

The fourth-day parallel seems less exact with Isaac; yet is he undoubtedly, more emphatically than any, the heavenly man. Even Abraham is found out of Canaan; Jacob almost spends his life away from it; Isaac may fail, and does, but never

---

*It has been noticed by many that the six days themselves fall into a double parallel series. Arranged thus, we have, as to the parts of creation touched on, these respectively:—

1. Light.	4. Light.
2. Waters.	5. Waters.
3. Earth.	6. Earth.

Dividing the third day into two will give us a regular series of seven, which is commonly in Scripture (as noted elsewhere) 4 *plus* 3.

leaves it; and as the picture of Christ Himself, as
he undoubtedly is, he is necessarily the picture of
the reflection of Christ—of the Son and of the
sons of God.

The parallel of the fifth-day type with Jacob is
self-evident; the lesson of each is *discipline*, and
what God accomplishes in it for His own—the
peaceable fruit of righteousness in those who are
exercised thereby.

While Joseph's life is as plainly the spontaneous
fruit of the new nature, and the attainment of
sovereignty over all around, as the sixth day is
also of the same things, none the less blessed because so little known.

Thus the remarkable unity of this first book of
Scripture is apparent. Nor will this glance at it
be in vain, if it awake in any soul a fresh realization of that eternal love so manifestly set upon us,
when He for whom are all things and by whom
are all things formed the heavens and laid the
foundations of the earth. Well may our voices
mingle in that jubilee-song, "Praise ye the Lord
from the heavens; praise Him in the heights;
praise ye Him, sun and moon; praise Him all ye
stars of light; praise Him, ye heavens of heavens,
and ye waters that be above the heavens. Praise
the Lord from the earth, ye dragons and all deeps;
mountains and all hills; fruitful trees and all
cedars; beasts and all cattle; creeping things and
flying fowl; kings of the earth, and all people;
princes and all judges of the earth; both young
men and maidens; old men and children; let them
praise the name of the Lord, for His name only
is excellent; His glory is above the earth and
heaven."

Paradise.

WE have noted already that from the fourth verse of the second chapter is a distinct part, and gives us "God in relationship with the creature He has made." Thus He is now spoken of, not simply as God—Elohim, but as *the Lord* God—Jehovah-Elohim.

Jehovah is the name of which the inspired translation is given in the third of Exodus—"I am:" expanded to its full significance in the book of Revelation as, "He which is, and which was, and which is to come." Thus in immutable existence He follows out the changes of created being, propping up creaturehood with the strength of eternity. "By Him all things consist." As in relation with a redeemed people—Israel—how blessed and reassuring this His covenant-name!

But here He is the "Lord God," not of Israel, but of *man*, a prophecy and picture of what shall be when "the tabernacle of God shall be with *men*." Still there is no "tabernacle of God" here; the final fact transcends all pictures.

That we have, however, a picture or type of eternal blessedness in this account that follows is plain to see. Its central figure, Adam, with his relationship to Eve, his wife, is so referred to elsewhere. (Rom. v. 14; Eph. v. 31, 32.) Paradise and the tree of life also meet us in prophecies of the blessedness to come. (Rev. ii. 7; xxii. 2.) That there should be contrast also in many respects is not inconsistent with the nature of types, but on the contrary most consistent. (1 Cor. xv. 45–48; Phil. ii. 6.) We may therefore in the beginning of things, contemplate the final end, however much we may find it true that "we see in part, and prophesy in part."

Man, then, is the manifest head of the new created scene; and if made in the image and likeness of God, how plainly is he in the image also of the true man, God's image. The dust of the earth, inspired by the breath of the Almighty, might well be the foreshadow of the union of the divine and human in one blessed Person in the time to come. The place of headship over all is but the anticipation of the wider headship of the Son of Man. "Image" and "likeness" of God have immeasurably fuller meaning in their application to the "last Adam" than to the first.

Then as to the relationship of the man and woman. It takes little to see in that "deep sleep" into which Adam was cast the figure of the deeper and more mysterious sleep of the "last Adam." Out of the man thus sleeping the woman is derived, as the Church out of Christ's death, and which by the creative Spirit is built up* as His body, "of His flesh and of His bones."

This building of the Church being not even yet complete, the presentation to Himself is of course still future. To that day, however, the apostle carries us on in thought, at the same time reminding us of the necessary contrast between the earthly first man and the heavenly second. For whereas the Lord God brought the woman to the man, "*He*"—the Second Man—shall "present unto *Himself*" the Church, "a glorious Church, not having spot or wrinkle or any such thing."

---

*The margin of Genesis ii. 22 gives rightly, for "*made* He a woman," "*builded*."

Our eyes are dim to see so far into the blessedness of that bright future which for eternity we
shall then enter on with Him. Let us rather turn
back here to see how distinctly it is noted that all
belongs of right to Him, whose love must needs
share it with His own. Thus, first of all, before
the Bride exists, the creatures are brought to
Adam, that he may see* what he will call them,
and as master of them all he gives them names.
And though the woman in due time shares this
sovereignty, as we know, (chap. i. 27, 28.) she yet
comes into it by her connection with the man,
and only so.

How perfect is the harmony of all this! How
blessed to see the Lord of heaven and earth
thus at the very beginning occupied with these
thoughts of His love as to that new creation
which was once again to be wrought out of the
ruins of the old! To wisdom such as this the craft
of Satan and the weakness of man could add
no after-thought. Against such power no other
power could be aught but as the potter's clay.
Such love combined with all gives acquiescence
and delight that all of power and all of wisdom
should be His, and make resistless the designs and
counsels of His heart.

And Eden, man's garden of delight! how sweet
to know that that which lingers lovingly yet in
the heart as in the traditions of men—which not
six thousand years of sin and misery have been
able utterly to banish from the memory—how
sweet to know that that also is but the type of a
far more blessed reality, "the Paradise," not of

---

*I do not doubt that "to see what he would call them," is that *Adam*
. might see.

man only, but "of God" (Rev. ii. 7.)! The little that we can say of it belongs rather to an exposition of Revelation than of Genesis. The trees and rivers and precious things of the latter we see but as images of beauty too little defined. It is to our shame, surely; for even as the fruits of the tree of life finally await the Ephesian "overcomer"—that is, the man who, amid the general decay and departure of heart from Christ, holds fast in the heart the freshness of the first, new-born love—so, who can doubt? a truer devotedness of heart to Him would give us even now a fuller knowledge, as well as a richer enjoyment, of what to Him (for it is His) the Paradise of God will be.

He who has the "keys of death and hell" has also, we may be sure, and in this sense too, the key of Paradise as well.

PART II.

DIVINE LIFE IN ITS VARIOUS ASPECTS.

Sec. 1.—Adam (Chap. iii.).

THE third chapter of Genesis is the real commencement of that series of lives of which, as is plain, the book mainly consists. It is where the first man ceases to be "a type of Him that was to come" that he becomes for us a type in the fullest way—figure and fact in one. The page of his life (and but a page it is) that treats of innocency is not our example who were born in sin. Our history begins as fallen, and so too the history of our new life in God's grace.

Figure and fact, as I have observed, are blended together here. We must be prepared for this, which we shall find in some measure the case all through these histories. Especially in this first one of all, what could be more impressive for us than the unutterably solemn fact itself? Children as we are of the fall, its simple record is the most perfect revelation that could be made of what we are in what is now our native condition, and also of how this came to be such. It is the title-deed to our sad inheritance of sin. And yet what follows in closest connection may well enable us to look at it steadfastly; for the ruins of the old creation have been, as we know, materials which God has used to build up for Himself that new one in which He shall yet find (and we with Him) eternal rest.

A simple question entertained in the woman's soul is the loss of innocence forever. It is enough only to *admit* a question as to Infinite Love to ruin all. This the serpent knew full well when he said unto the woman, "Yea, hath God said, Ye shall not eat of every tree of the garden?"—that is, Has God indeed said so? In her answer you can see at once how that has done its work. She is off the ground of faith, and is reasoning; and the moment reasoning as to God begins, the soul is away from Him, and then further it is impossible by searching to find Him out. Thus in Paradise itself, with all the evidence of divine goodness before her eyes, she turns infidel at once. "And the woman said unto the serpent, 'We may eat of the fruit of the trees of the garden, but of the fruit of the tree which is in the *midst* of the garden, God hath said, Ye shall not eat of it, *neither shall ye touch it*, LEST ye die.'"

Notice how plain it is that she is already fallen. She has admitted the question as to the apparent strangeness of God's ways, and immediately her eyes fasten upon the forbidden thing until she can see little else. God had set (chap. ii. 9.) the tree of *life* in the midst of the garden, and without any prohibition. For the woman now it is the forbidden tree that occupies that place. Instead of life, she puts death (or what was identified with it for her) as the central thing. The "garden of delight" has faded from her eyes. It has become to her the very garden of fable afterward* (where all was *not* fable, but this very scene as depicted by him who was now putting it before the enchanted gaze of his victim) in which the one

---

*The garden of Hesperides.

golden-fruited tree hung down its laden branches, guarded from man only by the dragon's jealousy. But here *God and the dragon had changed places.* Thus she adds to the prohibition, as if to justify herself against One who has lost His sovereignty for her heart, "Ye shall not eat of it, *neither shall ye touch it*"—which He had *not* said. A mere touch, as she expressed it to herself, was death; and why, then, had He put it before them only to prohibit it? What was it He was guarding from them with such jealous care? Must it not be indeed something that He valued highly?

She first adds to the prohibition, then she weakens the penalty. Instead of "ye shall surely die," it is for her only "*lest* [for fear] ye die." There is no real certainty that death would be the result. Thus the question of God's love becomes a question of His truth also. I do not want upon the throne a being I cannot trust; hence comes the tampering with His word. The heart deceives the head. If I do not want it to be true, I soon learn to question if it be so.

All this length the woman, in her first and only answer to the serpent, goes. He can thus go further, and step at once into the place of authority with her which God has so plainly lost. He says, not "Ye shall not surely die"—for so much the woman had already said—but "*Surely ye shall not* die." Her feeble question of it becomes on his part the peremptory denial both of truth and love in God: "Surely ye shall not die; for God doth know that in the day ye eat thereof, then your eyes shall be opened; and ye shall be as gods, knowing good and evil."

How sure he is of his dupe! and she on her

part needs no further solicitation: "And when the
woman saw that the tree was good"—she was
seeing through the devil's eyes now—"that the
tree was good for food"—there the lust of the
flesh was doing its work—"and that it was pleas-
ant to the eyes"—there the lust of the eyes comes
o_t—"and a tree to be desired to make one wise"
—there the pride of life is manifested—"she took
of the fruit thereof, and did eat; and gave also to
her husband with her, and he did eat."

Thus the sin was consummated. And herein
we may read, if we will, as clear as day, our moral
genealogy. These are still our own features, as in
a glass, naturally. Let us pause and ponder them
for a moment, as we may well do, seriously and
solemnly.

It is clear as can be that with the *heart* man first
of all *dis*believed. His primary condition was not,
as some would so fain persuade us, that of a seeker
by his natural reason after God. God had declared Himself in a manner suited to his condition,
in goodness which he had only to enjoy, and
which was demonstration to his every sense and
faculty of the moral character of Him from whose
hand all came to him. The very prohibition
should have been his safeguard, reminding the
sole master of that fair and gladsome scene, were
he tempted to forget it, that he had himself a
Master. Nay, would not the prohibited tree itself
have proved itself still "the tree of the knowledge
of good and evil," had he *respected* the prohibition,
by giving him to learn what sin was in a way he
could not else have known it, as "lawlessness,"
insubjection to the will of God?

The entertaining of a question as to God was,

as we have seen, man's ruin. He has been a ques-
tioner ever since. Having fallen from the sense
of infinite goodness, he either remains simply un-
conscious of it,—his gods the mere deification of
his lusts and passions,—or, if conscience be too
strong for this, involves himself in toilsome proc-
esses of reasoning at the best, to find out as afar
off the God who is so nigh. He reasons as to
whether He that formed the ear can hear, or He
that made the eyes can see, or He that gave man
knowledge know, or, no less foolishly, whether
He from whom comes the ability to conceive of
justice, goodness, mercy, love, has these as His
attributes or not! And still the heart deceives
the head : what he wills, that he believes. For a
holy God would be against his lusts, and a righteous God take vengeance on his sins; and how
can God be good and the world so evil, or love
man and let him suffer and die? Thus man reasons, taken in the toils of him who has helped him
to gain the knowledge of which he boasts,—so
painful and so little availing.

The way out of all this entanglement is a very
simple one, however unwelcome it may be. He
has but to judge himself for what he is, to escape
out of his captor's hands. Self-judgment would
justify the holiness and righteousness of God, and
make him find in his miseries, not the effect of
God's indifference as to him, but of his own sins.
It would make him also at least suspect the certainty of his own conclusions, which so many
selfish interests might combine to warp.

But still "Ye shall be as gods" deceives him,
and thus he will judge every thing, and God also,
rather than himself. And so, being his own god,

he becomes the victim of his own pride,—his god is his belly, as Scripture expresses it; insufficient to himself, and unable to satisfy the cravings of a nature which thus, even in its degradation, bears witness of having been created for something more, he falls under the power of his own lust, the easy dupe of any bait that Satan can prepare for him.

It is thus evident how the fall from God—the loss of confidence in divine goodness—is the secret of his whole condition,—of both his moral corruption and his misery together. For let my circumstances be what they may, if I can see them ordered for me unfailingly by One in whom infinite wisdom, power, and goodness combine, and whose love toward me I am assured of, my restlessness is gone, my will subjected to that other will in which I can but acquiesce and delight: I have "escaped the corruption that is in the world through lust," and I have been delivered from the misery attendant upon it.

To this, then, must the heart be brought back; and thus it is very simple how "with the *heart* man believeth to righteousness." The faith that is real and operative in the soul (and no other can of course be of any value), first of all and above all in order to holiness, works peace and restoration of the heart to God and, let me say, of *God* to the *heart*. How fatal, yet how common, a mistake to invert this order! And what an inlet of blessedness it is thus to cease from one's own natural self-idolatry in the presence of a God who is really (and worthy to be) that! There is *no such* blessedness beside.

But we must return to look at man's natural

condition. Notice how surely this leprosy of sin spreads, and most surely to those nearest and most intimate. Tempted ourselves, we become tempters of others, and are not satisfied until we drag down those who love us—I cannot say, whom we love, for this is too horrible to be called love—to our own level. Nay, if even we would consciously do no such thing, we cannot help doing all we can to effect it. We dress up sin for them in the most alluring forms; we invest them with an atmosphere of it which they breathe without suspicion. The woman may be here more efficient than the serpent. Herself deceived, she does not deceive the man, but she allures him. The victory is easier, speedier, than that over herself: "She gave also unto her husband with her, and he did eat."

The first effect is, "their eyes were opened;" the first "invention," of which they have sought out so many since, an apron to hide their shame from their own eyes. Thus conscience begins in shame, and sets them at work upon expedients, whereby they may haply forget their sins, and attain respectability at least, if conscience be no more possible.

How natural such a thought is we are all witnesses to ourselves, and yet it is a thing full of danger. It was the effort to retain just such a fig-leaf apron which sent the accusers of the adulteress out of the presence of the Lord. "Let him that is without sin among you cast the first stone at her" had been like a lightning-flash, revealing to themselves their own condition. They were "convicted in their own consciences;" but a convicted conscience does not always lead to self-judgment or to God: and "they, convicted by their own conscience, went out one by one, beginning at the eldest"—the one who naturally would have most character to uphold,—"even unto the last," and left the sinner in the only possible safe place for a sinner—in the presence of the sinner's Saviour. She, whose fig-leaf apron was wholly gone, who had no more character or respectability to maintain, could stay. This was what the loss of that still left to her; and so had He said to the Pharisees, "The publicans and harlots go into the kingdom of God before you." This is the misery still of man's first invention, which in so many shapes he still repeats.

When the voice of the Lord God is heard in the garden, the fig-leaf apron avails nothing. He hides himself from God among the trees of the garden: "I was afraid, because I was *naked*," is his own account. This is what alternates ever with self-justification in a soul: the voice of God —the *thought* of God—is terror to it. These two principles will be found together in every phase of so-called natural religion the world over, and they will be found equally wherever Christianity itself is mutilated or misapprehended, making their appearance again. Man, in short, untaught of God, never gets beyond them; for he never can quite believe that he has for God a righteousness that He will accept, and he never can imagine God Himself providing a righteousness when he has none.

Hence, fear is the controlling principle always. His religiousness is an effort to avert wrath,—in reality, if it might be, to get away from God: and even with the highest profession it may be, still "there is none that seeketh after *God*." Notice thus, the Lord's picture of the "elder son" in the parable, who, hard-working, respectable, no wanderer from his father, no prodigal, but righteously severe on him who has spent his living with harlots, finds it yet a service barren enough of joy. The music and dancing in the father's house are a strange sound to him: when he hears it, he calls a servant to know what it all means. His own friends, and his merriment, are all outside, spite of his correct deportment, and he speaks out what is in his heart toward his father when he says, "*Thou* never gavest *me* a kid, that I might make merry with my friends."

There the Lord holds up the mirror for the Pharisee of all time. Plenty of self-assertion, of self-vindication, even as against God Himself; the tie to Him, self-interest; his heart elsewhere; a round of barren and joyless services. This must needs break down in terror when God comes really in: indeed, the principle all through is fear, —servile, not filial.

So Adam hides himself among the trees of the garden, but the voice of the blessed God follows him. "And the Lord God called unto Adam, and said unto him, 'Where art thou?'"

Here, then, we begin to trace the actings of divine grace with a sinner. Righteousness has its way no less, and judgment is not set aside, but maintained fully. And herein is shown out the harmony of the divine attributes, the moral unity of the God whose attributes they are. There is no conflict in His nature. Justice and mercy, holiness and love, are not at war in Him. When He acts, all act.

Let us mark, then, first of all, this questioning of Adam on the part of God. Three several times we find these questions. He questions the man, questions the woman; the serpent He does not question, but proceeds instead immediately to judgment. Plainly there is something significant in this. For it cannot be thought that the Omniscient needed to know the things that He inquired about; therefore, if not for His own sake, it must have been for man's sake He made the inquiry. It was, in fact, the appeal to man for confidence in One who on His part had done nothing to forfeit it; the gracious effort to bring him to own, in the presence of his Creator, his present condition and the sin which had brought him into it. And it is still in this way that we find entrance into the enjoyed favor of a Saviour-God: "we have access *by faith* into this grace wherein we stand," the "goodness of God" leading "to repentance." Confidence in that goodness enables us to take true ground before God, and enables Him thus, according to the principles of holy government, to show us His mercy. Not in self-righteous efforts to excuse ourselves, nor yet in self-sufficient promises for the future, but "if we *confess our sins*, He is faithful and just to forgive us our sins, and to cleanse us from all unrighteousness."

To this confession do these questionings of God call these first sinners of the human race. Because there is mercy for them, they are invited to cast themselves upon it. Because there is none for the serpent, there is in his case no question. But let us notice also the different character of these questions, as well as the order of them. Each of these has its beauty and significance.

The first question is an appeal to Adam to consider his condition,—the *effect* of his sin, rather
than his sin itself. The second it is that refers
directly to the sin, and not the first. This double
appeal we shall find every where in Scripture.
Does man "thirst," he is bidden to come and drink
of the living water; is he "laboring and heavy-
laden," he is invited to find rest for his soul. This
style of address clearly takes the ground of the
first question. It is the heart not at rest here
rather than the conscience roused. Where the
latter is the case, however, and the sense of guilt
presses on the soul, then there is a Christ of whom
even His enemies testify that He receiveth sinners,
and whose own words are that the "Son of Man is
come to seek and to save that which is *lost*."

These are, as it were, God's two arms thrown
around men. Thus would He fain by every tie of
interest draw them to Himself,—of self-interest
when they are as yet incapable of any higher, any
worthier motive. How precious is this witness to
a love which finds all its inducement in itself—a
love, not which God *has*, but which He *is*! How
false an estimate do we make of it and of *Him*
when we make Him just such another as ourselves,—when we think of His heart as needing to
be won back to us, as if He had fallen from His
own goodness, with our fall from innocence! How
slow are we to credit Him when He speaks of the
"great love wherewith He loves us, even when we
are *dead* in sins"! How little we believe it, even
when we have before our eyes "God, in Christ,
reconciling the world unto Himself, not imputing
their trespasses unto them"! And even when the
awful cross, wherein man's sin finds alone its per-

fect evidence and measurement in one, manifests a grace overflowing, abounding over it,—even then can he justify himself rather than God, and refuse the plainest and simplest testimony to sovereign goodness, which he has lost even the bare ability to conceive.

In how many ways is God beseeching man to consider his own condition at least, if nothing else! In how many tongues is this "Adam, where art thou?" repeated to the present day! Every groan of a creation subject to vanity, whereof the whole frame-work is convulsed and out of joint, is such a tongue. And herein is Wisdom crying in the streets, even where there is no speech and no word, "So teach us to number our days, that we may apply our hearts unto wisdom." This, man never does until divinely taught. "Wisdom is justified" only "of her children."

And Adam does not yet approve himself as one of these. His confession of sin is rather an accusation of God.—"The woman whom Thou gavest to be with me, she gave me of the tree, and I did eat." In patient majesty, God turns to the woman. She, more simply, but still excusing herself, pleads she was deceived.—"The serpent beguiled me, and I did eat." Then, without any further question, He proceeds to judgment,—judgment in which for the tempted mercy lies enfolded, and where, if the old creation find its end, there appears the beginning of that which alone fully claims the title of "The Creation of God."

In the judgment of the serpent, we must remember first of all the essentially typical character of the language used. We have no reason to believe that Adam knew as yet the mystery of who the tempter was. "That old serpent, which is the Devil, and Satan," was doubtless for him nothing more than the most subtle of the beasts of the field which the Lord God had made. And herein, indeed, were divine wisdom and mercy shown, the tempter being not permitted to approach in angelic character, as one above man, but in bestial, as one below him; one indeed of those to which man as their lord had given names, and among which he had found no helpmeet. How great was thus his shame when he listened to the deceiver! he had given up his divinely appointed supremacy in that moment.

So in the judgment here it is all outwardly the mere serpent, where spiritually we discern a far deeper thing. "And the Lord God said unto the serpent, 'Because thou hast done this, thou art cursed among all cattle, and among all beasts of the field; upon thy belly shalt thou go, and dust shalt thou eat all the days of thy life.'" Thus the victory of evil is in reality the degradation of the victor: *he is degraded necessarily by his own success.* How plainly is this an eternal principle, illustrated in every career of villany under the sun! By virtue of it, Satan will not be the highest in hell, and prince of it, as men have feigned, but lowest and most miserable of all the miserable there. "Dust shall be the serpent's meat." "He feedeth on ashes: a deceived heart hath turned him aside, that he cannot deliver his soul, nor say, Is there not a lie in my right hand?"

But there is still another way in which the serpent's victory is his defeat:—"And I will put enmity between thee and the woman, and between thy seed and her seed; it shall bruise **thy head**, and thou shalt bruise His heel." That this last expression received its plainest fulfillment on the cross I need not insist upon. There Satan manifested himself prince of this world, able (so to speak) by his power over men to cast Christ out of it and put the Prince of life to death. But that victory was his eternal overthrow.—"Now is the judgment of this world; now shall the prince of this world be cast out; and I, if I be lifted up·from the earth, will draw all men unto *Me*."

This is deliverance for Satan's captives. It is not the restoration, however, of the old creation, nor of the first man. The seed of the woman is emphatically the "*Second* Man," another and a "last Adam," new Head of a new race, who find in Him their title as "Sons of God," as "born, *not* of blood (*i. e.*, naturally), nor of the will of the flesh, nor of the will of man, but of God."

This is not the place indeed for the expansion of this, for here it is not expanded. We shall find the development of it further on. Only here it is noted, that not self-recovery, but a deliverer, is the need of man ; and if God take up humanity itself whereby to effect deliverance, it must be the seed of the *woman*, the expression of feebleness and dependence, not of natural headship or of power.

The first direct prophecy links together the first page of revelation with the last, for only there do we find the full completion of it,—the serpent's head at last bruised. As a principle, the life of every saint in a world which "lieth in the wicked one" has illustrated and enforced it. In the next section of this book we shall return to look at this.

The judgment of the woman and the man now

follow, but they have listened already to the voice of mercy—a mercy which can turn to blessing the hardship and sorrow, henceforth the discipline of life, and even the irrevocable doom of death itself. That Adam has been no inattentive listener, we may gather from his own next words, which are no very obscure intimation of the faith which has sprung up in his soul. "And Adam called his wife's name Eve [life], because she was the mother of all living." The "woman which Thou gavest to be with me" is again "his wife," and he names her through whom death had come in, as the mother, not of the *dying*, but the living.

Thus does his faith lay hold on God,—the faith of a poor sinner surely, to whom divine mercy had come down without a thing in him to draw it out, save only the misery which spoke to the heart of infinite love. Like Abraham, afterward "he believed God," and while to the sentence he bows in submissive silence, the grace inclosed in the sentence opens his lips again. Beautifully are we permitted to see just this in Adam, a faith which left him a poor sinner still, to be justified, not by works, but freely of God's grace, but still put him thus before God for justification. And we are ready the more to apprehend and appreciate the significant action following: "Unto Adam also, and to his wife, did the Lord God make coats of skin, and clothed them." Thus the shame of their nakedness is removed, and by God Himself, so that they are fit for His presence; for the cover- ing provided of Himself must needs be owned as competent by Himself. And we have only to consider for a moment to discern how competent it really was.

Death provided this covering. These coats of skin owned the penalty as having come in, and those clothed with them found shelter for themselves in the death of another, and that the one upon whom it had come sinlessly through their own sin. How pregnant with instruction as to how still man's nakedness is covered and he made fit for the presence of a righteous God! These skins were fitness, the witness of how God had maintained the righteous sentence of death, while removing that which was now his shame, and meeting the consequences of his sin. Our covering is far more, but it is such a witness also. Our righteousness is still the witness of *God's* righteousness,—the once dead, now living One, who of God is made *unto us* righteousness, and in whom also *we* are made the righteousness of God. The antitype in every way transcends the type surely, yet very sweet and significant nevertheless is the first testimony of God to the Son;—a double testimony, first to the seed of the woman, the Saviour; and then, when faith has set its seal to this, a testimony to that work of atonement, whereby the righteousness of God is revealed in good news to man, and the believer is made that righteousness in Him.

Not till the hand of God has so interfered for them are Adam and his wife sent forth out of the garden. If earth's paradise has closed for them, heaven has already opened; and the tree of life, denied only as continuing the *old* creation, stretches forth for them its branches, loaded with its various fruit, "in the midst of the paradise," no longer of men, but "of God."

Sec. 2.—*The Carnal and Spiritual Seed.* (*Chap. iv., v.*)

IN the second part of this series we have a mingled story of two lives—of many individuals, but still only of two *lives*—essentially contrasted with one another. It is already the commencing fulfillment of that prophetic word which had spoken of the seed of the woman and the seed of the serpent. The story belongs, not to one generation only, but to every generation from that day to this; for while it is assuredly true that the real and fundamental victory which insures every other is His to whom belongs in its full sense the title of "Seed of the woman," yet it is true, too, that in every generation the great opponents have their representatives among men, and the conflict and the victory are in principle continually repeated.

The world has been from the beginning, as all history attests, a scene of unceasing strife; but its strife has been very generally a hopeless contest of evil with evil; for evil has no internal unity nor peace. Its elements may compact, but cannot concord. "Corruption is in the world through lust," lust is its essential feature, and we have had this already traced to its beginning in paradise itself; but lust means strife, means war, the conflict of jarring interests, each pursuing his own: "Whence come wars and fightings among you? Come they not hence, even of your lusts, which war in your members?" In such a collision there can be no true victory any where. Such history may fill men's chronicles; with God it is a mere unmeaning blank.

God's history is but the tracing, amid this darkness, of one silver line of light, light come into the world, a foreign element in it. With this the record of the six days' work begins: "Let there be light, and there was light." With this, too, begins the story of that of which we have already seen these creative days to be a type. We do not know how long the earth lay "waste and empty" under darkness; we do know that for man not long was the darkness unbroken. God's word again brought in light, although light at first long struggling with the darkness which it found; yet from the first God's benediction was its pledge of final victory. "Evening" might be, but not henceforth total "night;" while each "morning," as it follows, presages and brings nearer the full and perfect day, God's Sabbath-rest, when darkness shall be gone forever.

But here, then, is conflict, if mysterious, yet most real, where there are victories to be recorded, and where, thank God, the final victory is sure: a conflict just where the light is, and not elsewhere; a conflict to which every human heart in which God has spoken that out of darkness light may shine, is witness, and which is seen on a far grander scale in the field of the world at large. It is to this that the chapters now before us invite our attention; and as we shall see in these two spheres, where the inner world of the heart is but the miniature representative of the world without. We may see it more plainly if we trace it first upon the larger scale.

Here the blood of righteous Abel speaks to us of what often causes to the soul such deep perplexity, the apparent prevalence of evil over good:

a perplexity which is not removed until we see it as the law of the conflict we have spoken of. The seed of the woman shall bruise the serpent's head; but then the serpent shall first bruise the heel of the woman's seed. This applies first of all and pre-eminently, as already said, to Christ as the conqueror over man's mortal foe. In Abel's death we may thus see Christ, whose blood indeed speaks better things than that of Abel, but of whom Abel is none the less, as the first martyr, dying at a brother's hand, a perfect type.

If this be true, however, Cain must be a picture especially of the people, Christ's brethren, too, after the flesh, at whose hand he really died; and here at once the whole type assumes meaning and consistency.

Cain, then, is the Jew, the formal worshiper of God, bringing the work of his hands, the fruit of his own toil, not doubting that it ought to be accepted of God. Not irreligious, as men would say, he ignores the breach that sin had caused between man and his Creator, but of which the very toil whose fruit he brought was witness. So coming, he is necessarily rejected of God; and such is Pharisaism, of whatever grade or time. Just persons, having no need of repentance; diligent elder sons, serving the Father, but without getting so much as a kid to make merry with their friends; self-satisfied legalists, ignorant of God and grace: such is the Lord's picture of a generation of which Cain was prototype and father. Pharisees were they, who always were most zealous for commandments and against Christ, "going about to establish their own right-

eousness, and not submitting themselves to the
righteousness of God."

Abel, on the other hand, draws near to God,
bringing nothing of his own handiwork, but an
innocent victim, a life taken which no sin had
stained or burdened, a sacrifice most unreasonable
if it were not faith.   What pleasure could God
take in death? or how could the death of a guilt-
less substitute atone for the guilty?   Thus man
still reasons. But the very folly of Abel's sacrifice
to the eye of reason should suffice to assure us that
he was not following the promptings of his own
mind in it. His was not will-worship, but faith;
and if plainly the death of a beast could not take
away sin, his eye rested upon what that substitution foreshadowed. "By faith Abel offered unto
God a more excellent sacrifice than Cain." And
in this he might well speak to us of Him who, not
for Himself indeed, but as Man for men, offered
to God that one acceptable offering in which all
others find their consummation and their end.

"Witness" and "martyr" were from the beginning one. The self-righteous heart of Cain resents
the testimony to man's guilt and God's provision
for it, resents the testimony of God Himself to the
acceptance of Abel and his offering. In vain does
God graciously remonstrate with him; Abel is
slain, and Cain goes out from the presence of the
Lord, not to be slain of man, but to be a fugitive
and a vagabond upon the earth.

How like the people who bought Aceldama with
the blood of Christ—"the potter's field to bury
strangers in"! for the whole earth has been to
them since then a strangers' burial-ground. As
a vessel marred upon the wheel, they have been

witnesses for Him in their rejection that they are but as clay in the hands of Him against whom they have sinned.

Yet, though wanderers upon the earth, the nation subsists; for He who has ordained their punishment has also ordained its limit. They subsist with the mark of Cain upon them, a people who strikingly fulfill the character of Cain's progeny to this day, away from the presence of Jehovah, according to one of their own prophecies, "without a king, and without a prince, and without a sacrifice, and without an image, and without an ephod, and without teraphim."

With Lamech and his sons the line of Cain ends: one in whom self-will and impenitent abuse of God's long-suffering reach their height. A polygamist and would-be homicide, his name speaks of the human "strength" in which he rejoices, his wives' names of the lust of eye and ear after which he goes, his sons' names and their inventions of how, then as now, a soul away from God will use His creatures so as to be able to dispense with Him.* This is a generation such as those of whom the Lord said, "The latter end is worse than the beginning." With Cain, seven generations, and in the last still Cain, only developed further: progress in a race away from God, who will possess themselves of the earth in His despite, and be prosperous citizens in the land of vagabondage.

Happily this is not all; nor is that which is of

---

* Lamech is "strong;" Adah, "ornament;" Zillah, "tinkling" ("music-player" some interpret rather than translate it); Jabal, "the traveler;" Jubal, "the trumpet-blast;" Tubal-Cain is variously rendered, "worker in ore," "brass of Cain," "issue of Cain;" Naamah, "lovely."

God, though down-trodden, extinct upon earth. In Seth (appointed in the place of Abel, whom Cain slew) we have its resurrection, and henceforth its perpetuation. The line of Cain perished with the old world in the waters of the deluge; with Seth, God begins, as it were, the race of man anew (chap. v.), Cain and the fall being now omitted. Seth is the son of man, so to speak, in his likeness who was made in the likeness of God and blessed. With Seth, there are nine generations unto Noah, in whom once more the earth is also blessed: three triads, for God manifests Himself in as well as to His people; at the end of the second of which Enoch goes to heaven without seeing death, while Noah is God's seed, brought through the judgment to replenish and find his blessing on the earth beyond. The Church of first-born ones and Israel find here very plainly their representatives, to those who have learned from Scripture the respective destinies of each. Fittingly, therefore, does Enoch become the earliest prophet of the Lord's approach (Jude 14.), while the days of Noah are expressly likened, by the Lord Himself, to the time of the coming of the Son of Man.

The more we look, the more we shall see the force of the comparison. Infidelity has invited our attention to a correspondence between the two lines of Cain and Seth, and there is a certain correspondence which it will be well to examine. The resemblance of some names pointed out is no doubt superficial; but there are undoubtedly two Enochs and two Lamechs, and the latter close upon the end of the old world. Of the two Enochs, all that is noted is but contrast. The first gives his name to the city which Cain builds as it were in defiance of his sentence, a city whose builder and maker God is *not*. Enoch, one of a line which have no earthly history, walks with God, and is not, for God has taken him. The two Lamechs have more in common, for alas! the separateness which at first obtained between the worshipers of Jehovah and those in alienation from Him narrowed as time went on. It was when Enos was born that men began to call upon the name of the Lord, for "Enos" is "frail" or "mortal man," and those content to bear that title learn the mercies of a covenant-keeping God. But as time goes on, Lamech succeeds to Enos—strength to weakness, the world and the Church approach; and thus Lamech, like his Cainite representative, has his memorable saying also: pious, and largely true, but with one fatal flaw in it. Lamech called his son's name "'Noah,' saying, 'This same shall comfort *us* concerning our work and toil of our hands because of the earth which the Lord has cursed.'"

And the comfort came, and in Noah, real blessing for the earth from God. Lamech was thus far a true prophet; but the people to whom he spoke, or the survivors of them, with their whole posterity, save Noah's family alone, *were all cut off by the flood that preceded the blessing*.

Is there nothing similar now, when boundary-lines are nearly effaced, and the Church has shifted from the Enos to the Lamech-state, and peace is preached in the assurance of good days coming, while intervening judgment, universal for the rejecters of present grace, is completely ignored and set aside?

Seth's line has warning as well as comfort for us, then; yet is it after all the line to which God's promise and His blessing cleave, and while the world profits naught by their inventions, it is beautiful to see how He numbers up the years of their pilgrimage. With them alone there is a chronology, for He who telleth the stars "numbers their steps" and "telleth" even "their wanderings."

Thus far, then, as to the interpretation of this primeval history as it applies to the larger scale of the world around. But there is a world within which corresponds certainly not less to what these types signify, and which lies apparently yet more within the scope of these Genesis biographies. In this inner world, wherever God has wrought, the same conflict is found, and subject to the same laws. Through death, life; through defeat, victory.

In this sphere of the individual experience the conflict is between two natures—the one which is ours as born naturally; the other, as born of God supernaturally: and here, evidently, the order is, "first, that which is natural, and afterward that which is spiritual." The law of Genesis is thus that the elder gives place to the younger. Cain represents, therefore, that in us which we rightly and necessarily call "the old nature." His name signifies "acquisition, possession;" Abel's, "vapor, exhalation." The contrast between them cannot be questioned, and was prophetic of their lives: Cain possessing himself of that earth on which for man's sake the curse rested, while Abel's life exhaled to God like vapor drawn up by the sun. We may be very conscious, as Christians, of these opposite tendencies: the "flesh," so designated because in it man is sunk down from the spiritual being, which he was created, into mere "body," as we may say, or dust, while the new nature rises Godward.

Not that the flesh cannot have a religion of its own. It can bring its offering Cain-wise, the fruit of a toil which should convict it as outside of paradise, and (expecting it to be received, of course,) be roused to anger by not finding the tokens of acceptance which a mere prodigal, coming home as that, obtains;—the spirit of him who was, again, "the *elder* son," and who, while professing, "Lo, these many years do I serve thee, neither transgressed I at any time thy commandments," had still to add, "and yet thou never gavest me a kid, that I might make merry with my friends." How many of those even in whom there is begun in the heart some true desire after God, are yet destitute of all knowledge of acceptance with Him, because they are endeavoring to approach Him after Cain's pattern, taking their own thoughts instead of His! Faith still, taught of His Word, brings Abel's offering—the surrender of a life unstained by sin, and yielded therefore on account of others, not its own; and faith is the character and expression of the new nature: we arc "all the children of God by faith in Christ Jesus."

The interpretation of the type runs smoothly so far. The difficulty will be for most that Abel should die, and by his brother's hand—a difficulty quite parallel to that which it represents, that when we have so begun to live, we should find in practical experience a law of sin overmastering, death in the place of life.—"For I was alive with-

out the law once, but when the commandment
came, sin revived, and I died."—"For sin, taking
occasion by the commandment, deceived me, and
by it slew me."

Thus, while it is surely true that the life which
as children of God we partake of cannot be slain,
it is nevertheless true *as to experience*, from which
side the type presents things here, that it is after
we have begun to live the true and eternal life we
have to learn what death is—to pass through the
experience of it in our souls, and learn deliverance
from "the body of this death."

In the struggle with evil, we too (though in a
very different way from Him who alone is fully
and properly the woman's seed) find victory from
defeat.   We need, on our own account (as He did
not), the humiliation of it.   Jacob, though heir of
blessing, must halt upon his thigh before he
can be Israel, a prince with God; and what
seems on the one side to be unredeemed evil
and its triumph only, shall in another be found
the mighty and transforming touch of the "angel
that redeems from evil."

We must have the sentence of death in ourselves,
that we may not trust in ourselves, but in God that
raiseth the dead.   The possession of life—of the
new nature—is not power over sin; and this we
have to learn, that all "power is of God."   Trust
in a new nature which we have got is still trust in
ourselves as having got it; and self-confidence in
whatever shape is still a thing alienate from God,
and to be broken down, not built up.   We must
come to the self-despairing cry, "Who shall deliver
me from the body of this death?" before we can
learn, as we shall then surely learn, to answer,

"I thank God, through Jesus Christ our Lord."

Thus Abel dies, and Cain lives and flourishes; away from God indeed, but not permitted to be slain. The flesh abides in us, though we are born again; we cannot destroy it when we gladly would. Nay, we have, before we can find the fruit we seek for, to see the flesh in its fruit, under its fairest forms, the evil thing it ever was. To its seventh generation, "that which is born of the flesh is flesh,"—from Cain to Tubal-cain, "Cain's issue." But then we have reached a new beginning, and for other fruit find another tree—Seth, appointed of God as a seed "in the place of Abel, whom Cain slew."

Just so when the fruits of the flesh are manifest, and we have proved the inefficacy of the right and good desires which come of the new nature in us: when we have failed to work deliverance for ourselves, and have had to cry in despair, "O wretched man that I am! who shall deliver me from the body of this death?" we find the answer in a fruitful seed bestowed in place of Abel—"I thank God through *Jesus Christ* our Lord," and the "law of the Spirit of life *in Christ Jesus*" makes us "free from the law of sin and death;"—not "the life," but "the *Spirit* of life,"—not our effort, but divine might,—not self-occupation, but occupation with Him in whom we are before God, and in whom the divine favor rests upon us full and constant as upon Him (and *because* on Him) it rests. "I, yet not I, but Christ in me." This is a second substitution which for deliverance it imports a soul to know: the substitution of the power of the Spirit for the power of a right will and human energy, the substitution therefore of occupation with Christ for occupation with holiness; for then and thus alone is holiness attainable.

From Seth, then, "Enos" springs.* We can take home the sentence of death; we can glory in weaknesses, that the strength of Christ may rest upon us; and His power known—the living God for us, as we find Him whom our weakness needs, we "worship God in the Spirit, and rejoice in Christ Jesus, and have no confidence in the flesh." "Then began men"—from the birth of Enos— "to call upon the name of the Lord."

And with Seth, Adam's line begins afresh, as if sin had never entered, as if it had never blotted the page of human history. Like the genealogy in Luke, where, the Son of Man having come in, Adam again shines forth in the brightness of his creation as "the son of God;" so here begin once more "the generations of Adam," with no record of the fall to touch the blessed fact that "in the day that God created man, in the likeness of God made He him." No Cain, *nor even Abel*, enters here. The record is of a life in all its generations not of this world, yet the days of which in the world God numbers: a life which is fruitful, but whose fruit it is not yet the time to show; a life to which alone is appended the record of a walk with God, and which not only finds its home with God in Enoch, but with Noah also, in due time, after the long-suspended judgment is poured out, inherits the earth also by perpetual covenant of a covenant-keeping God.

---

* "Frail" or "mortal man."

Sec. 3.—*Noah.* (*Chap. vi.–xi.* 9.)

(1.)—*Chap. vi.–ix.* 17. To Noah's life, as a type, the third chapter of the first epistle of Peter is the key. His bringing through the flood is there declared to be a type of "salvation," but salvation of a fuller kind than ordinarily is reckoned such. The figure is a simple one enough to follow in the main, and will itself guide us if we cleave closely to it.

For, plainly, the ark is Christ, and the flood it saves through is the judgment of the whole world, which perished in it, while those preserved are brought through to a new world which emerges from the waters, and where the sweet savor of accepted sacrifice secures a perpetuity of blessing.

It is the third stage of new life as apprehended by the soul, resurrection therefore, as bringing in the place of which it is said, "If any man be in Christ, [it is] new creation: old things are passed away; behold, all things are become new;"—words which remarkably correspond to Noah's position as come through the flood, making allowance for that essential inferiority of type to antitype which we have often had to refer to as a necessary principle for true interpretation.

Noah is evidently not the type of a sinner, taken up as such, nor could he be, to stand in the place he does in these biographies. He is a just man, a Cornelius rather, a type of those who, quickened and converted though they be—"fearing God and working righteousness"—need yet to know the salvation which the gospel brings.

In the world around, corruption is total and universal. The judgment of the whole is pronounced, with one way of escape, and only one, left open to the man of faith.

The ark is built of gopher-wood. We know not this "gopher," but the resemblance is remarkably close to the "copher" or "pitch" named afterward, and the resemblance has been noticed by many. On account of it the gopher has been of old believed to be the cypress, and might well have furnished the "pitch" also for the vessel's seams.* The type would thus correspond more fully to the antitype, for there need be no doubt but that the gopher, like the shittim-wood of the tabernacle-ark, refers to Christ, while "copher" is the word used elsewhere for "atonement." That the tree should be cut down to provide a refuge from the waters of judgment was not enough, the seams must be pitched with the pitch the tree supplied. And so death, as mere death, even though Christ's, would not have been enough to put the soul in security that fled to Him for refuge. The only blood, as the apostle teaches, that could be carried into the presence of God for sin, was the blood of a victim burned without the camp.† The place of distance due to the sinner and the unclean had to be taken by the Holy One of God, in order to our salvation.

In such an ark we, with Noah, may make "nests" (for so, instead of "rooms," the margin more literally reads). The love that has provided all gives more than security; the house of refuge is not

---

*For there seems no scriptural proof or otherwise of "copher" being b.tumen, although the Septuagint and Vulgate translate it so, and most modern interpreters follow these.

†And here, *upon the ground*—without an altar. The altar, as what "sanctifies the gift," is doubtless the person of the Lord, as what gave value to His work; but in the sin-offering the altar is not seen, for the Victim stands in the sinner's place, and is treated as if He were *not* the Person that He really is.

mere bare walls; amid the very storm of judgment the heart that craves may find its lodgment where more than a father's care, more than a mother's tenderness, are found.

The door of the ark was in the side, but the window above.‡ It is no new thing to say that this is faith's outlook. The passengers in that marvelously guided and protected vessel needed not their eyes for pilotage, and were not to look out upon the solemnities of the judgment taking effect around; while the waters, which were the grave of the world, floated them above its mountain-tops up to the blue heavens, calming as they rose. What a season for them—shut in by God, with God! and what a preparation for commencing that new life which they were to begin in the world beyond the flood!

And many may recall a not less solemn time, when they too, having fled for refuge from the storm of coming wrath, were made to pass through the world's judgment, and to find in Him who, dead for them and risen, has passed into the heavens, their own escape, not from judgment merely, but from the whole scene of it. They have come in Christ through the floods which fell on Him alone, and in Him have reached a "*new* creation," old things passed away, and all things become new.

For even Christ (as the apostle tells us) we know no more after the flesh. Plainly, the only Christ there is to know is one no more found among men; and if our being "in Him" means any thing, it

---

‡ This has been contested, but seems undoubtedly the meaning of the passage. And it is confirmed by the fact that not till Noah removed the covering of the ark could he see that the ground was dry.

means this: identification with Him who stands as really for us in the glory of the heavens as once for us He hung upon the cross.

It must be remembered that not sense nor experience brings us there. Even Noah may have heard or seen little, if any thing, of that which he passed through; but none the less real was that eventful passage. For us, faith alone can make us realize a plan as to which "eye hath not seen, nor ear heard, neither have entered into the heart of man" what nevertheless the Spirit of God through the Word has revealed to us. We are there (if in Christ) apart from all experience; and what experience we are to have of it will be the fruit of, and in proportion to the vigor of, our faith alone.

The ark grounds upon the mountains of Ararat, and not long afterward occurs the well-known incident of the raven and the dove. As a type, this shows us how little is forgotten or denied in these Genesis-biographies, what we practically are, conscious as we may be of our place in Christ Jesus. Saved out of the world, and no more of it, we yet carry with us and may let out the raven. We have that in us which can take up with a scene of death from which the waters of judgment have not yet dried up, and like the unclean bird use the ark but as a means of pursuing with the more vigor its congenial occupation.* Noah first sends forth the raven, but, as others have noted, he distrusts it and sends forth the dove; but the dove finds no rest for the sole of her feet, and returns unto him into the ark. Seven days after, she goes forth again, and returns with an olive-leaf, the assurance of peace and of the fruitfulness of the new world.

---

*"Went forth, going and returning" (viii. 7, marg.) seems to indicate this,

Shortly after, but at the word of God, and not at the suggestion of his own mind, Noah goes forth, and the first-fruits of the place into which he has been brought is an altar from which the smoke of a burnt-offering goes up,—a savor of rest to Jehovah. Neither altar nor burnt-offering have we had before, and who can doubt the suitability of their first mention here? for the altar is the person of Christ—that which gave its value to His blessed work, and the burnt-offering is that aspect of His work in which its value Godward is most fully shown. And here, in the new-creation scene pictured for us in this chapter, surely we know in a new way and with a new blessedness, not merely salvation, but the Saviour; and not merely the human side of that salvation—its result for *us*, but its divine side—its Godward result. The knowledge of the salvation sets us free to be occupied with the Saviour; and He who cannot be known now after the flesh (for He is risen and with God) can only be apprehended justly when we have been brought from off the ground of the world that rejected Him, to find our true place where He is,—in the light, where He is the light, and the glory in His face is the true test and discovery of all else.

"And Jehovah smelled a savor of rest; and Jehovah said in His heart, I will not again curse the ground any more for man's sake, for the imagination of man's heart is evil from his youth; neither will I again smite any more every thing living, as I have done." Thus the hopelessness of expecting any thing on man's part, which was before the flood the reason for his judgment, is now, through the efficacy of accepted sacrifice, but a reason for setting man aside altogether as a hindrance of blessing and of establishing it in perpetuity upon an unchangeable basis. The new creation thus abides forever in bloom and beauty of which the earth under the Noachian covenant is but indeed a "shadow."

The heirs of this inheritance find next their own blessing. Their fruitfulness is certainly not more an injunction than a gift of the grace which is now manifesting itself for them (ix. 1.). And so in what these types speak of.

Then their authority over the lower creatures is restored: the fear and dread of man is to be upon every beast of the earth, and upon all that moves, and they are delivered into his hand. All things are his, and even death itself is now to furnish him with food. This is a fact of the deepest significance; it is death ministering to life, a principle of which God would keep us in constant remembrance. Scarcely a meal but thus testifies to us of the very basis of all real gospel, which the Lord's supper fully and formally declares. But it is only after known deliverance, and in the new place with God that this can be rightfully understood. We now go farther than the type, and overpass the restriction here imposed: *we drink the blood also;* that which is God's only as atonement (for "it is the blood that maketh atonement for the soul") is ours to sustain and cheer us as atonement *made.* "The cup which we bless, is it not the communion of the blood of Christ?"

Thus are they set in the fullness of blessing: delivered, brought into a scene secured to them irrespective of their own desert, fruitfulness assured sovereignty of the whole bestowed, and death itself put into their possession and made to minister to their sustenance with all else. And now comes in, in its due and fitting place, the question of responsibility to judge the deeds of the flesh, for which before they were incompetent. When Cain shed his brother's blood, in the old world now passed away, God set a mark upon Cain, lest any one finding him should kill him; whereas now, in this new world, God speaks far otherwise: "And surely your blood of your lives will I require; at the hand of every beast will I require it, and at the hand of man. Whoso shed-deth man's blood, *by man* shall his blood be shed; for in the image of God made He man."

This is evidently the principle of all human gov-ernment, which began from this date, established by God Himself. We have its history shortly epitomized for us in Noah's weakness and want of *self*-government, which exposes him to the scorn of those whom he should have governed; and on the other hand, in Nimrod, high-handed power, abused to satisfy the lust of ambition and self-will. Yet the powers that be are ordained of God, while for the abuse of power, or for the inability to use it, they are accountable to Him.

On the other side of the flood also (in the typical sense) we are set in authority, for the use of which we are responsible to God. Power is in our hands from God to judge the deeds of the flesh, which before deliverance we could not judge, and to vin-dicate the image of God in which we have been created. And to this is appended once more the blessing of fruitfulness, which, however it be of God and of grace, is yet not possible to be at-tained where nature is unjudged.

Lastly, the covenant is ratified, and a token given to confirm it. The bow in the cloud is man's assurance; but it is more, it is God's memorial of the new relationship into which He has entered with His creatures. *His* eye, and not man's only, is upon the bow, and thus He gives them fellowship with Himself in that which speaks of peace in the midst of trouble, of light in the place of darkness; and what this bow speaks of it is ours to realize, who have the reality of which all figures speak.

"God is light," and "that which doth make manifest is light." Science has told us that the colors which every-where clothe the face of nature are but the manifold beauty of the light itself. The pure ray which to us is colorless is but the harmonious blending of all possible colors. The primary ones—a trinity in unity—from which all others are produced, are, blue, red, and yellow; and the actual color of any object is the result of its capacity to absorb the rest. If it absorb the red and yellow rays, the thing is blue; if the blue and yellow, it is red; if the red only, it is green; and so on. Thus the light paints all nature; and its beauty (which in the individual ray we have not eyes for) comes out in partial displays wherein it is broken up for us and made perceptible.

"God is light;" He is "Father of lights." The glory, which in its unbroken unity is beyond what we have sight for, He reveals to us as distinct attributes in partial displays which we are more able to take in, and with these He clothes in some way all the works of His hands. The jewels on the High-Priest's breastplate—the many-colored gems whereon the names of His people were engraved

were thus the "Urim and Thummim "—the "Lights
and Perfections," typically, of God Himself; for
His people are identified with the display of those
perfections, those "lights," in Him more unchangeable than the typical gems.

In the rainbow the whole array of these lights
manifests itself, the solar rays reflecting themselves
in the storm; the interpretation of which is simple.
"When I bring a cloud over the earth," says the
Lord, "the bow shall be seen in the cloud; and I
[not merely you] will look upon it." How blessed
to know that the cloud that comes over our sky is
of *His* bringing! and if so, how sure that some
way He will reveal His glory in it! But that is
not all, nor the half; for surely but once has been
the full display of the whole prism of glory, and
that in the blackest storm of judgment that ever
was; and it is this in the cross of His Son that God
above all looks upon and that He remembers.

Still the principle is wider, and in every season
of distress He does surely at last display His glory.
At last the storm is banded with the brightness;
and this too is a token of the covenant of God with
His people that not destruction, but their blessing,
His nearer manifestation and their better apprehension of it, is the meaning of the storm.

(2.)—*Chap. ix.* 18–*xi.* 9. The story of the deliverance closes here, and we now come to a very
different, in many respects a contrasted, thing—
the history of the delivered people. The history
begins with failure; it ends with confusion, and
from the gracious hand that but now delivered
them. It is the humbling lesson of what we are,
but which we have now to read in the light of

what He is. This will make indeed the shadows
deeper, but we can face them in the knowledge
that God is light and in Him no darkness; and
that for us, too, "the darkness is passing, and the
true light already shines."

First, Noah fails, the natural head of all; and sin
thus afresh introduced propagates itself at once in
his family, and becomes the curse of Canaan and
his seed. Noah's snare is the abundance of the
new-blessed earth, a thing not easy to understand
typically until we see (what will be more fully before us when we come to Abraham's life) that it is
the earthly side of the heavenly life we have to do
with in the succeeding histories. Thus Abraham
is *in Canaan* as a pilgrim and a stranger, a thing
that in our Canaan (for no one doubts, I suppose,
what Canaan means) is an absolute impossibility;
yet the earthly side is pilgrim and strangership,
and the two things thus linked together derive a
meaning from their connection they would not
have alone. Just so with Noah; the earth side of
the typical heavenly life is Nazariteship, and Noah
falling from his Nazariteship exposes himself to
his shame. The fall tests his children, as the presence of sin still tests the spirit of those who deal
with it. Ham in further exposing it to his brethren reveals himself, not taking it as his own, while
Shem and Japheth cover, without looking upon,
their father's nakedness. "Ham" is "black,"—the
unenlightened—or perhaps rather the "sun-burnt,"
—scorched and darkened by the very light itself;
for light, if not received as light, becomes a source
of darkness to the soul. And Ham is the father of
Canaan,—the "trader," as his name imports. The
parentage of evil in the professing church seems

thus traced, even as in the world before the flood, to one who goes out from the presence of the Lord, only darkened and branded by the light in which he had found no pleasure. Canaan is in the professing church its fruit—the trader in divine things, who may be found in the land, and even in the "house of the Lord," but every-where true to his unhappy character: "bondsman of bondsmen," and no free-born child of light, he is finally driven out of the house which he has made a den of thieves, and finds his true place in Babylon the Great, whose "merchants are the great men of the earth."

Of Noah's two other sons we seem to read in their various blessing two tendencies which are apt to be sundered, and should not. Shem's is the recipient contemplative life, whose danger it is to run into the mystical; Japheth's, the practical, energetic life, which in its one-sidedness tends to divorce itself from faith. In the blessing of Shem, it is Shem's God, Jehovah, who is blessed, as it is indeed the highest blessedness of faith that it has God for its portion and its praise; while Japheth's blessing is in enlargement, and in dwelling in Shem's tents, for the practical life finds its home in faith alone, and true service is but worship in its outflow toward men.

Of the genealogies which follow in the tenth chapter I shall say—can indeed say—little. We may notice that the Egyptian (Mizraim) is also a son of Ham, the darkness of nature (as we speak) being not so much defect of, as *resisted*, light. The Philistines, too, are Egyptians, as we may by and by more consider. Then Nimrod, the son of Cush, the ' rebel," as his name imports, the beginning of whose kingdom is in Babel, points too plainly to the apostate king of the last days to admit much question. Let us now proceed, however, to look at Babel itself, with the account of which this section closes. Here, without doubt, too, Babylon the Great is pictured, although not in the full development in which we look at it in Revelation xvii, xviii.

The account is remarkable for its clearness and simplicity. The process by which the professing church settled down in the world, and then built up for itself a worldly name and power, could scarcely be more fully or in plainer terms described. How with one consent they turned their backs upon the sunrise (2 Pet. i. 19.), and leaving the rugged and difficult places in which they were first nurtured—too painful for flesh and blood—descended to the easier if lower level of the world,* —how settling there, ease and abundance wrought in them desire to possess themselves in security of the earth and make themselves a name in it; how Babylon thus was built, "a city," after Cain's pattern, whose builder and maker God was *not*, and a "tower" of strength, human and not divine; all this he that runs may read. Let us notice further, that this is a carnal imitation and anticipation of God's thoughts, and that thus the earthly city usurps the titles and prerogatives of the heavenly one. But Babylon cannot be built of the "living stone," which is the God-made material for building; they have moved from the quarries of the hills, and must be content to manufacture less durable "brick" out of the mere clay which the plain

---

*The meaning of Shinar is considered uncertain. Among others possible is that of "waking sleep," which would at least be very appropriate.

affords: they have brick for stone and slime (or bitumen) for mortar—*i. e.*, not the cementing of the Spirit, the true Unifier, but the worldly and selfish motives which compact men together, and are but fuel for the fire in the day "the fire shall try every man's work of what sort it is."

This was what makes a figure in men's histories —the Catholic Church of antiquity, singularly one indeed, whether you look at it in Alexandria or Constantinople or Rome, were most fully developed. The unity whereof it boasted was not God's, and if God came down to see what man was building, it was not to strengthen, but to destroy—not to compact, but scatter. The many tongues of Protestantism are but His judgment upon the builders of Babel; its multitudinous sects but the alternative of the oppressive tyranny with which when united she laid her yoke upon the minds and consciences of men, and under which the blood of the saints ran like water. They are but a temporary hindrance, moreover, for when the antitypical Nimrod shall make it the beginning of his kingdom, Babylon shall sit as a queen, anticipating no widowhood and no sorrow. Then, however, her doom shall be at hand, "in one day shall her plagues come upon her."

Sec. 4.—*Abraham.* (*Chap. xi.* 10–*xxi.*)

(I.) His Path. (*xi.* 10–*xiv.*)—The life of Abraham is the well-known pattern-life of faith, as far as the Old Testament could furnish this. It connects, as already noticed, in the closest way, with the story of Noah which precedes it, and alone makes it possible. For the essential characteristic of the life of faith is strangership, but this founded upon citizenship elsewhere. Faith dwells in the unseen, substantiating to itself things hoped for. This is exemplified in Abram, called to Canaan, his possession in hope alone. He dwells there, but in tabernacles, the bringing together of two things typically—the heavenly calling and its earthly consequence. Canaan is here Noah's new world beyond the flood, and, as we all know, heaven; but the earthly aspect of this is, as all through Genesis, the prominent one. We must wait for Joshua before we get a distinct type of how faith lays hold, even now, of the inheritance in heaven. Here, tent and altar are as yet the only possession.

The introduction to this history is the record of Abraham's descent from Shem. It is a record of failure, of which the whole story is not told here, for we know that his line whose God Jehovah was were worshiping other gods when the Lord called Abraham from the other side of Euphrates (Josh. xxiv. 2.). The genealogy itself may tell us something, however,—in Peleg, how men were possessing themselves more than ever of the earth, and at the same time the days of their tenure of it shortening rapidly,—by half, in this very Peleg's time (comp. ch. x. 25.). Reu lives two hundred and thirty-nine years; Serug, two hundred **and thirty;**

Nahor, but one hundred and forty-eight; Terah, again, two hundred and five; but Haran dies before his father Terah. God yet numbers the fleeting years of those who have forgotten Him.

Now we find a movement in Terah's family, the full explanation of which we must look for outside of Genesis. Here, it seems to originate with Terah, for we read that "*Terah* took Abram his son, and Lot the son of Haran, his son's son, and Sarai his daughter-in-law, his son Abram's wife; and they went forth from Ur of the Chaldees, to to go into the land of Canaan: and they came unto Haran, and dwelt there." Terah fulfills his name ("delay"), and ends his days at Haran, so called from his dead son. Natural things hold him fast, though death be written on them, and memory but perpetuates his loss. "Haran" means "parched," yet there he abides (and Abram with him) till he dies. Then we find that whom he had led he had been holding back; and Abram rises up in the power of a divine call which had come to him, and to him alone in the first place, and by which he was separated from country, kindred, and father's house alike, to be blessed and a blessing in the land pointed out of God for his abode. And now there is no further delay: "they went forth to go into the land of Canaan, and into the land of Canaan they came."

Which of us does not know something of these compromises, which seem to promise so much more than God and to exact so much less, but in which obedience to God goes overboard at the start, and which end but in Haran, and not Canaan? Who would not have thought it gain to carry our kindred with us, instead of a needless and painful separation from them? Why separate, when their faces can be set in the same way as ours? and why not tarry for them and be gentle to their weakness, if they do linger on the road? How hard to distinguish from self-will or moroseness and unconcern for others, the simplicity of obedience and a true walk with God! But the lesson of this is too important to end here, and Lot's walk with Abraham is yet to give us full-length instruction upon a point which is vital to the life of faith.

But now Abram is in the land. We hear of the first halt at Sichem (Shechem), at the oak of Moreh. The first of these words means "shoulder," the second, "instructor;" and it is in bowing one's shoulder to bear that we find instruction. He that will do God's will shall know of the doctrine: he that will learn of Christ must take His yoke. This is the "virtue" in which still is "knowledge" (2 Pet. i. 5.). The oak of Moreh grows at Shechem still.

And it is surely "in the land" we find it: power for full obedience in those heavenly places, where we are "blessed with all spiritual blessings," and where "to the principalities and powers are made known by the Church the manifold wisdom of God." It is as Canaan-dwellers the secrets of God's heart are opened to us; and Christ, in whom we are, becomes the key of knowledge as of power. In Him, "in whom dwelleth all the fullness of the Godhead bodily," we are "filled up."

Jehovah now appears to Abram, and confirms the land to his seed as their inheritance; and here for the second time in Genesis we read of an "altar," the first that Abram builds. He worships in the fullness of blessing, and then first also his "tent" comes into view: "he removed from thence into a mountain on the east of Bethel, and *pitched his tent*, having Bethel on the west, and Hai on the east." "Hai" means "a heap of ruin," and is the city which in Joshua resists the power of Israel, after Jericho falls to the ground. It is as if the very ruins of Jericho had risen up against those who had lost the victorious presence of God their strength. Typically, Hai is no doubt the ruined old creation, and thus between a judged world and the "house of God" Abram's tent is pitched, in view of both. Here, too, once more he builds an altar, and calls upon Jehovah's name.

But Canaan is a dependent land. It is contrasted with Egypt as not being like it watered with the foot, but drinking directly of the rain of heaven.* And although the eyes of the Lord are there continually, that does not exclude the trial which a life of faith implies and necessitates. Thus Abram finds a famine in the land to which God has called him, and to avoid it goes down to Egypt. There it becomes very evident that he is out of the path of faith, and he fails openly.

But we must note that the secret failure had begun before, and the famine itself had followed, not preceded this. A famine in Canaan cannot be *mere* sovereignty on God's part—sovereign though He be. And thus we find that when Abram, fully restored in soul, returns to the land, it is "to the place of the altar, which he made there at the

---

* Egypt of course must needs be dependent also, but not so immediately. Its river was its boast, and the sources of supply were too far off to be so easily recognized: a vivid type of the world in its self-sufficiency and independence of God. They are yet sending scientific expeditions to explore the sources of their unfailing river; and by searching yet have not found out God.

first." There, between Bethel and Hai, he had been at the beginning; but there he had not been when the famine came, but in the south—his face toward Egypt, if not yet there. This border-land is ever a dry land, and Abram found it so. Famine soon comes for us in our own things when we get into this border-land. But who that has known what God's path is but has known the trial of a famine *there?* And when we find such, how Egypt tempts—how the world in some shape solicits to give up the separate place which we have taken. Few, perhaps, but have made some temporary visit to Egypt in the emergency. But the price of Egypt's succor is well known. Abram's fall there has been but too constantly repeated, and its repetition upon the largest scale has been one great step in the failure of the whole dispensation. Sarai in Pharaoh's house is but the commencement of that which reaches its full development in the guilty commerce of the harlot-woman with the kings of the earth. But the germ is yet very different from the development, and Sarai is of course by no means the apocalyptic woman. She is, as the epistle to the Galatians tells us, the covenant contrasted with the Sinaitic, as grace with law. The grace in which we stand God has linked with faith, and with faith alone. It belongs not to the world in any wise. We are not of the world: "we are of God, and the whole world lieth in wickedness." But who can maintain that testimony, when the world's help is wanted, and association with it sought? It is evident some form of universalism must be preached. Sarai (grace) must not be held as Abraham's exclusive possession, but the world allowed to believe it can

obtain what divorced from faith is sufficiently attractive to it. Give Sarai up, and you shall have
wealth and honors—be the king's brother-in-law;
and by simony such as this has the Church bought
peace and prosperity in the world; but the world
will yet learn by judgment (as did Pharaoh) that
Sarai is not its own. This manifest, its favors
cease, and Abram is sent away.

And now the true character of Lot comes out.
His story (one of the saddest in Genesis) is most
important to be noticed in a day when, God having revealed to us the truth of our heavenly calling, it is but even too plain that there are many
Lots. The word "Lot" means "covering," and
under a covering he is ever found. With Abraham
outwardly, he is not at heart what Abraham is;
and with the men of Sodom outwardly, he is not
after all a Sodomite either. He is a saint, and
therefore not a Sodomite, though in Sodom. He
is a saint untrue to his saintship, and herein Abraham's contrast, even of his companion. His is,
however, alas! a downward course. First, with
Abraham, a pilgrim; then, a dweller in Sodom;
finally, he falls under deeper personal reproach,
and his life ends as it began—under a covering.
There is no revival, no effort even upward,
throughout nothing but mere gravitation, drag-
ging down into still deeper ruin lives associated
with his. His wife's memorial is a pillar of salt; his
daughters', a more abiding and perpetual infamy,
linked with his own shame forever. How terrible
this record! How emphatic an admonition to remember, in him, how near two roads may be at the
beginning which at the end lie far indeed apart!
Reader, may none who read this trace this by-path,

save here where God has marked out for us the
end from the beginning, that with Him we may
see it; not, as having trod it, the beginning from
the end.

The beginning is found here:—

" And Terah took Abram his son, *and Lot the son
of Haran, his son's son* . . . to go into the land of
Canaan; and they came unto Haran, and dwelt
there."

Nature, taking in hand to follow a divine call,
which it had never understood nor heard for itself;
leading without being led; settling down short altogether of the point for which it started, to dwell
in a scene of death to which it clings spite of dis-
satisfaction:—these are the moral elements amid
which many a Lot is nurtured. Terah shines out
in him when, having undertaken to walk with
Abram, the plain of Jordan fixes his eyes and
heart; once again, when in the presence of judgment, the messengers of it laid hold upon his hand,
the Lord being merciful to him, and brought him
forth and set him without the city,—because " he
lingered."

But there is another beginning, after this; for
now—

"*Abram* took Sarai his wife, *and Lot his brother's
son*, . . . and they went forth to go into the land
of Canaan, and into the land of Canaan they came."

Not nature now, but the man of faith leads, and
they no longer linger on the road; but Lot merely
follows Abram, as before he had followed Terah.
Abram walks with God; Lot only with *Abram*.
How easy even for a believer to walk where another's bolder faith leads and makes the way practicable, without exercise of conscience or reality

of faith as to the way itself! How many such there are, practically but the camp-followers of the Lord's host, adherents of a cause for which they have no thought of being martyrs, nearly balanced between what they know as truth and a world which has never been seen by them in the light of it. For such, as with Lot, a time of sifting comes, and like dead leaves they drop off from the stem that holds them.

Egypt had acted thus for Lot. The attraction it had for him comes out very plainly there where the coveted plain of Jordan seems in his eyes "like the land of Egypt." But beside this, it is easy to understand how Abram's failure there had loosened the moral hold he had hitherto retained upon his nephew. Yet still true to the weakness of his character, Lot does not propose separation, but Abram does, after it was plain they could no longer happily walk together. Their possessions, increased largely in Egypt, separate them, but Abram manifests his own restoration of soul by the magnanimity of his offer. Lot, though the younger, and dependent, shall choose for himself his portion; and he, not imitating the unselfishness by which he profits, lifts up his eyes and beholds the fertility of the plain of Jordan, and he chooses there.

The names unmistakably reveal what is before us here. Jordan ("descending") is the river of death, flowing in rapid course ever down to the sea of judgment, from which there is no outlet—no escape.* There, in a plain soon to be visited with fire and brimstone from the Lord, he settles down,

---

* The Dead Sea, it is well known, lies in a deep hollow, twelve hundred and ninety-two feet below the level of the Mediterranean, and there is no river flowing out of it.

at first still in a tent though among the cities there, but soon to exchange it for a more fixed abode in Sodom, toward which from the first he gravitates.

Lot-like, even this he covers with a vail of piety. The plain of Jordan is "like the garden of the Lord"—like paradise: why should he not enjoy God's gifts in it? He forgets the fall, and that paradise is barred from man, argues religiously enough, while under it all the real secret is found in this: It is "like the land of Egypt." How much of man's reasoning comes from his heart and not his head—a heart too far away from God! It is significantly added, "As thou comest unto Zoar;" and thus indeed Lot came to it.

But Abram dwells in the land of Canaan, and God bids him walk through it as his own. Thereupon he removes and dwells in Mamre ("fatness") which is in Hebron ("companionship, communion"). The names speak for themselves again sufficiently. May we only know, and live in, the portion of Abram here.

In the next chapter things are greatly changed. Abram himself is in connection with Sodom, as well as with another power, which we may easily identify as essentially Babylonish. The names are difficult to read, and two at least of the confederated countries are just as doubtful.* But in the first enumeration Amraphel, king of Shinar, stands first, the undoubted representative of the kingdom of Nimrod, although Chedorlaomer appears the most active and interested. They all seem but

---

* For the attempt to make Ellasar Hellas, or Greece, though favored by the Septuagint, can scarcely be maintained. It is more probably Larsa. Nor is Tidal, king of nations, a very satisfactory representative of the Roman power, as some take it.

divisions of this Babylonish empire however, though changed no doubt into a confederacy of more or less equal powers.

These *four* kings—and our attention is specially called to the number here (ver. 9.)—are at war with the *five* petty kings of the plain of Jordan. Typically, these last represent the world in its undisguised* and sensual wickedness; the Babylonish kings, the religious world-power, always seeking to hold captive (and in general successfully) the more open form of evil. Indeed the Sodom of heathenism never yielded but to a spiritual Babylon which had already obtained supremacy over the Christianity of Scripture and the apostles; and in no way was this last ever really established, nor could it be. But the world craves some religion; and nothing could suit it better than one which with external evidences to accredit it, such as undeniably historical Christianity had, linked its blessings with a system of ordinances by which they could be dispensed to its votaries. This exactly was the character of Nicene Christianity, and hence its conquest of the Roman empire. The leaven was already in the meal: the adulteration of the gospel had already advanced far; but leaven (evil as in Scripture its character undoubtedly is) has certainly the power of rapid diffusion, and rapidly the popularized gospel spread.

These, then, are the powers represented here. The portion of Abram lies outside the whole field of conflict. Lot, on the other hand, is already in Sodom, and of course is carried captive in the captivity of Sodom. It is the spiritual history of those

---

* Undisguised indeed, if Gesenius is right as to Bera being equivalent to Ben-ra, "son of evil," and Birsha to Ben-resha, "son of wickedness."

who, having known the truth, fall under the power
of the world-church which Babylon represents.
It is their link with the world by which they are
sucked in. And such is the secret of all departure
from the truth. The Lord is too faithful to allow
mere honest ignorance to be deceived; and although men may credit Him with it, the record
still stands: "Whosoever willeth to do His will
shall know of the doctrine, whether it be of God."

The secret of Abram's power is revealed in one
pregnant word, which as here used of him flashes
light upon the scene before us: "There came one
that had escaped, and told Abram the *Hebrew*."
That word, patronymic as it may be, is yet significant: it means "the passenger." So Peter exhorts
us, "*as* strangers and pilgrims, to abstain from
fleshly lusts"—the destruction of Sodom, while to
the pilgrim, Babylon, claiming her kingdom now
in the yet unpurged earth, can only be the perse-
cutor, "red with the blood of the saints and of the
martyrs of Jesus." Here may seem a difference
between Abram and the spiritual sons whom he
represents; but *typically* he none the less may represent those who, after their Lord's example, con-
quer by suffering. There never were more real
conquerors than were the martyrs.

So Abram brings back his brother Lot and all
the other captives; whose deliverance indeed was,
as we see, merely incidental. For as between
Sodom and Shinar how could Abram interfere, or
what deliverance would it be for a mere child of
Sodom to be delivered from the power of Babylon?
Even as to Lot it is once more solemnly made manifest that not circumstances have made him what
he is, and that change of circumstances do not

change him. Freed by God's hand work ng by
another, he is not really free; and soon we shall find
him needing once more to be delivered from what,
having escaped man's judgment, falls under God's.

But if Lot's eyes are still on Sodom, those of his
pilgrim-brother find another object. For as he
returned from the slaughter of the kings, "Melchisedek king of Salem brought forth bread and
wine; and he was the priest of the Most High
God." The type is explained to us by the apostle
in the epistle to the Hebrews; and we all know in
Christ the Priest after the order of Melchisedek.
The apostle's words are remarkable for the way in
which they bring out and insist upon the perfection of Scripture, in what it omits as well as what it
inserts. "Without father, without mother, without
beginning of days or end of life," are words which
have been thought to show that the mysterious
person before us was no other than Christ Himself;
but this the apostle's very next words disprove;
for "*made like* unto the Son of God" could not be
said of the Son of God Himself. It is simply of
the omissions of the narrative that the apostle is
speaking; these omissions being necessary to the
perfection of the type. He is our High-Priest, not
finding His place among the ephemeral generations of an earthly priesthood, but subsisting in
the power of an endless life; Priest and King in
one. Whilst, however, the Lord is thus even now
a Priest after the *order* of Melchisedek, it is not
after Melchisedek's pattern that He is now acting.
Here, His type is rather Aaron. It is at a future
time—a time, as we say, millennial—that He will
fulfill the type before us, as many of its features
clearly show. Thus Melchisedek is priest of the

Most High God,—a title always used of God in the coming day of manifested supremacy. This Melchisedek's own words show: "Blessed be Abram of the Most High God, Possessor of heaven and earth." The interpretation of his name, and the name of his city, confirms this: "First of all, 'King of Righteousness'; and after that, 'King of Salem,' which is, 'King of Peace.'" This is the order in which the prophet gives the same things, when speaking of millennial times: "Then judgment shall dwell in the wilderness, and righteousness remain in the fruitful field; and the work of righteousness shall be peace, and the effect of righteousness, quietness and assurance forever."

His place in this chapter is in perfect and beautiful keeping with all this. For we find the timeliness of Melchisedek's appearance to the victor over the kings, when the king of Sodom says to Abram, "Give me the persons, and take the goods to thyself." It is to the "Most High God, Possessor of heaven and earth"—the One of whom Melchisedek has spoken to him,—that Abram declares he has lifted up the hand, not to take from a thread even to a shoe-latchet. Christ seen thus by the pilgrim man of faith, claiming on God's part all that is his own, is the true antidote to the world's offers. If Christ could not accept the kingdoms of the world at the hands of Satan, but from His Father only, no more can His followers accept enrichment at the hands of a world which has rejected Christ for Satan. And that bread and wine which we receive from our true Melchisedek, the memorial of those sufferings by which alone we are enriched, for him who has tasted it, implies the refusal of a portion here.

(2) ABRAHAM'S INNER LIFE. (*ch. xv.–xxi.*)—It is evident that in the fifteenth chapter we have a new beginning, and that we pass from the more external view of his path and circumstances to that of his inner life and experiences. Abram is now for the first time put before us as a man righteous by faith, a thing fundamental to all spiritual relationships and all right experiences. It was not, surely, now for the first time that he believed the Lord when God said to him under the starry sky of Syria, "So shall thy seed be." Yet here it pleased God first openly to give the attestation of his righteousness: words which lay for a gleam of comfort to how many sin-tossed souls, before God could come openly out with the proclamation of it as His principle, that a "man is justified by faith without the deeds of the law."

There are two things specially before us in this chapter; and they come before us in the shape of a divine answer to two questions from the heart of Abram. The two questions, moreover, are drawn out of him by two assurances on God's part, each of which is of unspeakable moment to ourselves.

The two assurances are, (1) "Fear not, Abram; I am thy shield, and thy exceeding great reward;" (2) "I am the Lord that brought thee out of Ur of the Chaldees, to give thee this land to inherit it." As we would read this for ourselves now,—"God is our portion," and "Heaven is the place in which we are to enjoy our portion."

To the first assurance Abram replies, "Lord God what wilt Thou give me, seeing I go childless?" to the second, "Lord God, whereby shall I know that I shall inherit it?" Strange words, it may seem, in the face of God's absolute assurance;

yet questions which do speak to us of a need in
man's heart which not merely God's word, but
God's act must meet; questions which thus He
takes up in His grace, seriously to answer, and
that we through all time may have the blessedness
of their being answered.

The answer to both, no Christian heart can
doubt, is Christ; for Christ is God's answer to
every question.   Here it may be figuratively and
enigmatically given, as was characteristic of a
time in which God could not yet speak out fully.
None the less should it be plain to us now what is
intended, and unspeakably precious to find Christ
unfolding to us, as it were, out of every rose-bud
in this garden of the Lord.

"*After these things* the word of the Lord came
to Abram in a vision: 'Fear not, Abram: I am
thy shield, and thy exceeding great reward.'"

Had Abram been fearing?   The things that had
just transpired, and to which the Lord evidently
refers, were his victory over the combined power
of the kings, which we have already looked at;
and secondly, his refusal to be enriched at the
hands of the king of Sodom.   Brave deeds and
brave words! wrought with God and spoken before God, who could doubt?   Yet it is nothing
uncommon, just when we have wrought something,
for a sudden revolution of feeling to surprise us,—
for the ecstatic and high-strung emotion upon
whose summit we were just now carried, to sub-
side and leave us, like a stranded boat, consciously,
if we may so say, above water-mark.   The necessity of action just now shut out all other thought.
That over, it no longer sustains.   We drop out of
heroism, to find—what?   Blessed be His name!—

God Himself beneath us! We who were shielding others find more than ever the need of God our shield: we who were energetically refusing Sodom's offers need to be reminded, "I am thy exceeding great reward." Thank God, when the boat strands there!

God our defense! what shaft of the enemy can pierce through to us? God our recompensing portion! what is all the world can give? In this place of eternal shelter, oh to know more the still unsearchable riches!

"Of Christ," adds the apostle. Did not Abram feel the lack of our revelation there,—unintelligent as he may be as to what was wanted, and utterly unable, of course, to forestall God's as yet but partially hinted purpose? Grasping, as it were, at infinity, and unable to lay hold of it, he drops from heaven to earth, and cries, with something like impatience, as the immensity of the blessing makes itself felt in his very inability to hold it, "Lord God, what wilt Thou give me, seeing I go childless, and the steward of my house is this Eliezer of Damascus? . . . . Behold, to me Thou hast given no seed; and, lo, one born in my house is mine heir."

How flat all God's assurances seem to have fallen with the pattern man of faith! And yet we may find, very manifestly, in all this our pattern. It is all very well to say that Abram's faith was not up to the mark here. In truth it was not; but that is no explanation. Do you know what it is, apart from Christ as now revealed to us, to grasp after this immensity of God your portion? If you do, you will know how the wings of faith flutter vainly in the void, and cannot rise to it. Thank God, if you cannot rise, *God can come down;* and so He does here to Abram. Serenely He comes down to the low level of Abram's faith, and goes on to give him what it can grasp: "And, behold, the word of the Lord came unto him, saying, 'This shall not be thine heir; but he that shall come forth out of thine own bowels shall be thine heir.' And He brought him forth abroad, and said, 'Look now toward heaven, and tell the stars, if thou be able to number them: so shall thy seed be.' And he believed in the Lord; and He counted it to him for righteousness."

The many seeds and the One are here; and the many to be reached by means of the One. Abram's "One Seed" must be familiar to us all. Through and in Isaac we read Christ: "He saith not, And unto seeds, as of many; but as of one, 'And to thy Seed,' which is Christ." To us, at least, is it an obscure utterance of how this first assurance is made good to us, and possible to be realized? The Son of Man, here amongst us, where faith shall need no impossible flights to lay hold of Him, and the infinity of Godhead shall be brought down to the apprehension of a little child. Himself "the Child born," Himself the "Son given," the kingdom of peace is forestalled for those with whom, all the faculties of their soul subdued and harmonized under His blessed hand, "the calf and the young lion and the fatling" dwell together, and a little child leads them.

God our shield, and God our reward: we know these, we appreciate them in Him who is God manifest, because God incarnate.

The second question now comes up.—"And He said unto him, 'I am the Lord that brought thee out of Ur of the Chaldees, to give thee this land to inherit it.' And he said, 'Lord God, whereby shall I know that I shall inherit it?'"

Here too the question is plain, and to be answered by deeds, not words. The land for us is the good land of our inheritance, the land upon which the eyes of the Lord are continually—not earth, but heaven. A wonderful place to enjoy our portion, when we know indeed what our portion is! "Where I am" is the Lord's own description; and thus you will find it most apt and suited, that it is not until *He* stands before us upon earth that the full clear revelation of an inheritance in heaven is made to us. *He* uncloses heaven who ascending up there carries the hearts of His disciples within its gates. Did they open to admit us without this, would not our eyes turn back reluctantly to that earth only familiar to us? Did they not open now, would they not be an eternal distance-putting between us and our Beloved? "That where I am, there ye may be also" explains all. The stars *shining out of heaven* are thus in this chapter the evident symbol of the multitudinous seed.

But *how* is man to reach a land like this? A place with Christ, reader! Look at what you are, and answer me: what is to raise a child of earth up to the height of God's own heaven?

No work of man, at least; no human invention of any kind. How could we think of a place with Christ as the fruit of any thing but God's infinite grace? He who came down from the glory of God to put His hand upon us, alone can raise us up thither. No human obedience merely, even were it perfect, could have value of this kind, because it would be still merely what was our duty to do. He to whom obedience was a voluntary

stooping, not a debt, alone could give it value.
And He, raised up from the dead by the glory of
the Father, and gone in as man into the presence
of God, brings us for whom His work was done
into the self-same place which as man He takes.

Thus God answers Abram by putting before
him Christ as the pledge of inheritance: "Take
Me a heifer of three years old, and a she-goat of
three years old, and a ram of three years old, and
a turtle-dove, and a young pigeon." God delights
to accumulate the types of what Christ is, and
press their various significance upon us. These
are all types which are brought out more distinctly
before us in the offerings after this. The three
beasts—all tame, not wild, nor needing to be cap-
tured for us, but the willing servants of man's
need; each three years old—time in its progress
unfolding in them a divine mystery. The first
two, females, the type of fruitfulness: the heifer,
of the patient Workman; the she-goat, of the Victim for our sins; the ram, in whom the meek surrender of the sheep becomes more positive energy,
—afterward, therefore, the ram of consecration,
and of the trespass-offering. (Lev. v. 15; viii. 22.)
The birds speak of One from heaven, One whom
love made a man of sorrow (the turtle-dove), and
One come down to a life of faith on earth (the
rock-pigeon, like the coney, making its nest in the
place of security and strength).

To unfold all this, and apply it, would require a
volume. No wonder, for we have here our occupation for eternity begun. These, the fivefold type
expressed in one perfect Man, Abram "divided in
the midst, and laid each piece one against another,
but the birds divided he not; and when the fowls

came down upon the carcasses, Abram drove them away." Thus upon all these types of moral beauty, and that they may be fit types of Him whom they represent, death passes, and they lie exposed under the open heaven, faith in Abram guarding the sacrifice from profanation, until, "when the sun was going down, a deep sleep passed upon Abram, and he slept; and, lo, a horror of great darkness fell upon him." Faith's watchfulness is over; darkness succeeds to light; but this only brings out the supreme value of the sacrifice itself, which not faith gives efficacy to, but which sustains faith. God Himself, under the symbol of the "smoking furnace and the burning lamp," passes between the pieces, pledging Himself by covenant* to perform His promise of inheritance. Purifier and enlightener, He pledges Himself by the sacrifice to give the discipline needed in faith's failure, and the needed light in the darkness it involves; and thus the inheritance, not apart from the suited state to enjoy it with God, but along with the conditions which His holiness (and so His love) necessitates.

How complete and beautiful is this, then, as the answer to Abram's second question! If, with his eyes upon himself, he asks, "How shall I know that I shall inherit it?" he is answered by the revelation of the infinite value of all that puts a holy God and a righteous One, in both characters, upon his side: underpropping faith in all its frailty, and securing holiness as fully as it secures the inheritance itself. These types and shadows belong assuredly to us, to whom Christ has become the revelation of all, the substance of all these shad-

*See Jeremiah xxxiv. 18, where God announces the doom of those who had not performed the covenant made with Him, when they "cut the calf in twain, and passed between the parts thereof."

ows. Ours is indeed a wider and a wondrous inheritance. But so ours is a sacrifice of infinite value, and which alone gave their value to these symbols themselves. How precious to see God's eye resting in delight upon that which for Him had such significance, ages before its import could be revealed! How responsible we whom grace has favored with so great a revelation!

Thus all is secured to Abram by indefeasible promise on the ground of sacrifice. It is of promise as contrasted with law, as the apostle says. Abram believes the promise, but does not yet know this contrast. He believes God, but not yet simply; alas! as with all of us at the beginning, he believes *in himself* also. He is a believer, but not yet a circumcised believer. Do you perchance even yet know the difference, beloved reader? It is this that Abram's history is to make plain to us.

"Now Sarai, Abram's wife, bare him no children." Sarai is, as we have seen, the principle of grace, and this is one of the strangest, saddest things in a believer's experience, the apparent barrenness of that which should be the principle of fertility in his life and walk. "Sin shall not have dominion over you, because ye are not under the law, but under grace." And yet it is the justified man, and who thus far at least knows what divine grace is, who says, "When I would do good, evil is present with me;" and "The good that I would I do not; but the evil that I would not, that I do." It is impossible to read the lesson of the seventh of Romans aright until we have seen this. The struggle that it speaks of is not a struggle after peace or justification; nay, cannot

be known aright until this is over. The whole
secret of it is the break-down, not of a sinner, but
of a saint. That efforts after righteousness before
God should be vain and fruitless is simple enough;
but that efforts after holiness should be fruitless is
a very different thing, and a much harder thing to
realize. It is *Sarai's* barrenness that troubles us.
Alas! how in this distress Sarai herself, as it were,
incites us to leave her; persuading us, she may be
builded up by Hagar!

Of Hagar also we have the inspired interpretation. She is the covenant "from the mount Sinai,
which gendereth to bondage:" the only form of
religion that man's natural thought leads him to,
and that to which, if grace is left, we necessarily
drop down. Hagar is thus an Egyptian, a child
of nature, or as the epistle to the Galatians interprets, "the elements of the world." The principle
of law, however much for the purposes of divine
wisdom adopted by God, was never His thought.
He uses it that man being thoroughly tested by it
may convince himself by experiment of the folly
of his own thoughts. It is thus Sarai's handmaid,
though exalted often even by the man of faith to a
different place. The tendency of law, as it were,
to depart from this place of service is shown in
her very name—Hagar, that is, "fugitive;" and
thus the angel of the Lord finds her by the well,
going down to Egypt. When she is finally dis-
missed from Abram's house, she is again found
with her son, gravitating down to Egypt; and
upon the wilderness upon its borders Ishmael
dwells afterward. How little Christians suspect
this tendency of that by which they seek holiness
and fruit! Yet even that which, as given by God,

is necessarily "holy and just and good," speaks nothing of heaven or of Christ, or, therefore, of pilgrim-life on earth.   But thus all of power is left out also; for Abram's pilgrim-life springs from his Canaan-place; and "in Christ Jesus neither circumcision availeth any thing nor uncircumcision," —the whole condition of man as man,—"but a new creation."

Abram takes Hagar, however, to be fruitful by her, just as believers in the present day take up the law simply as a principle of fruitfulness, not at all for justification: it is their very thought that is being tested here.   And the effect at first seems all that could be desired: fruit is produced at once.   It is only when God speaks that it is seen that Ishmael is, after all, not the promised seed. The immediate result is, Sarai is despised: "And when she saw that she had conceived, her mistress was despised in her eyes."   So it ever is.   Once admit the principle of law, and what is law if it be not sovereign?   Faith may cling to and own barren Sarai still, but the principle introduced is none the less its essential opposite.   "Sarai dealt hardly with her," and "she fled from her face."

The scene that follows in the wilderness is, I doubt not, a lesson from the dispensations.   It is the instruction, not of experience, as in Romans, but, as in Galatians, of divine history.   It is the explanation of the divine connection with the law. It is between the promise of the seed and its fulfillment that Hagar's history comes in.   The law was given, not from the beginning, but four hundred and thirty years after the promise was made; and it was added till the Seed should come to whom the promise was made.   Again, it was not God

who first gave Hagar to Abram, but Abram who
took Hagar: that the experiment might be worked
fully out, God sends her back to him; that is all.
So in like manner the covenant at Sinai was not
God's own proper thought, but what was in man's
mind taken up of God to be worked out, under
true conditions, to its necessary result. The whole
scene is here significant: God's own voice now
recognizing, and insisting on, that servant-place
which alone Hagar filled; the "fountain of water"
by which Hagar is found, the symbol of that spiritual truth which, connected with law, is not law;
that characterizing, before his birth, of the "wild-
ass man," Ishmael—child of law, and lawless,—just
as the law from the beginning foretold its own necessary issue: "Every imagination of the thought
of man's heart" being "only evil, and that continually." Therefore the vail before the holiest, and
the declaration, even to Moses, "Thou canst not
see My face." God in all this, we may note, appears to Hagar, and *not to Abram:* for thirteen
years more we read of no further intercourse between God and Abram.

But "when Abram was ninety years old and
nine, the Lord appeared unto Abram, and said
unto him, 'I am the almighty God; walk before
Me, and be thou perfect.'" This is the period to
which the apostle refers in the epistle to the Romans, when his body was now dead, being about
one hundred years old; and it is striking to see
how completely the intermediate years from the
taking of Hagar are counted but as loss. "And
being not weak in faith, he considered not his own
body now dead, when he was about a hundred
years old, neither yet the deadness of Sarah's

womb: he staggered not at the promise of God through unbelief; but was strong in faith, giving glory to God; and being fully persuaded that what He had promised He was able also to perform: *and therefore it was imputed to him for righteousness.*" (Rom. iv. 19–22.)

Now here it should seem as if the apostle had confounded times far apart. It was at least fourteen years before that Abram had "believed in the Lord, and He counted it to him for righteousness." Before Ishmael was born his body was not dead, for Ishmael was born "after the flesh," or in the energy of nature merely, in contrast with the power of God. It could not have been at that time, then, that he considered not his body now dead. Thus the faith that the apostle speaks of is really the faith of the later period. All the intervening time is thus covered, and the two periods brought together.

Natural power had to reach its end with him before the power of God could be displayed. It was now an almighty God before whom Abram was called to walk. Mighty he had known Him; not really till now *al*mighty. The apprehension of power in ourselves limits (how greatly!) the apprehension of so simple a fact as that all "power belongeth unto God." By our need we learn His grace; by our poverty, His fullness; and the Christian as such has to receive the sentence of death in himself, that he may not trust in himself, but in God that raiseth the dead, and as a child of Abraham find his place with God according to the covenant of circumcision.

"For we are the circumcision, who worship God in the Spirit, and rejoice in Christ Jesus, and have no confidence in the flesh;" "having put off the body of the flesh by the circumcision of Christ." The cross is our end as men in the flesh, not that we should trust in ourselves now as Christians, but in Christ: that as we have received Christ Jesus our Lord, we should walk IN HIM. How little is it realized what that is! In our complaints of weakness, how little that to be really weak is strength indeed!

What comfort is there for us in the fact that thus "sprang there of one, and him as good as dead, so many as the stars of the sky in multitude, and as the sand which is by the sea shore innumerable"! How serious and how blessed that upon all the natural seed is the very condition upon which alone they can call him father! the token of the covenant was to be in his flesh for an everlasting covenant, the token of the perpetual terms upon which they were with God. How striking to find that under the law the very nation in the flesh must carry the "sign of circumcision, a seal of the righteousness of the faith which Abraham had being yet uncircumcised"! and that at any time, spite of the middle wall of partition still standing, any Gentile could freely appropriate the sign of such a righteousness, and with his males circumcised sit down to the feast of redemption— the passover-feast!

Another reminder is here: "And he that is eight days old shall be circumcised among you, every man-child in your generations, he that is born in the house, or bought with money of any stranger, which is not of thy seed." Every child of God is both born in the house and bought with money; not with silver and gold, but with the precious blood of Christ, as of a lamb without blemish and without spot: and the "eight days old" shows to how fair an inheritance we are destined; for the eighth day speaks, of course, to us of new creation, the first week of the old having run out.   It is in the power of the knowledge of this that practical circumcision can alone be retained.   In the wilderness Israel lost theirs, and on reaching Canaan had to be circumcised the second time.   So too the water of separation had to be sprinkled on the third day: in the power of resurrection only could death be applied for the cleansing of the soul. The sense of what is ours in Christ alone qualifies us to walk in His steps.   It is only what His own words imply,—"Abide in Me, and I in you.   As the branch cannot bear fruit of itself except it abide in the vine, no more can ye except ye abide in Me."   "As ye have received Christ Jesus the Lord, walk ye in Him."

Abraham.

CIRCUMCISION known, we find in the next chapter God in communion with Abraham (now indeed Abraham) after a manner never before enjoyed. The Lord not only comes or appears to him, but openly associates Himself with him as with one of whom He is not ashamed. No one can doubt, that looks at it, the suggestive contrast with the next chapter, in which Lot for the last time comes before us, the very type of one "saved so as through the fire." This has been seen by others, but the more we look at it, the more striking and instructive will it be found. I shall dwell at more length than I have usually permitted myself upon lessons of such intense and practical interest as are those which God in His mercy has here given us.

It should be evident that the foundation of all this contrast expresses itself in the different position of these two men—the one, in the door of his tent at Mamre; the other, in the gate of Sodom. In the one, we see still the persistent pilgrim; in the other, one who has been untrue to his pilgrimship, and is settled down amid the pollutions of a sinful world. Striking it is, and most important to remember, that he is a "righteous man," expressly declared so by the word of inspiration: "That righteous man, in seeing and hearing, vexed his righteous soul from day to day with their ungodly deeds." He is thus an example of how "the Lord knoweth how to deliver the godly out of temptations." (2 Pet. ii. 7, 9.) This is a complete contrast with the way in which the book of Genesis represents him. I need scarcely say, there is no contradiction; and the contrast itself is a very beautiful

instance of the style of Scripture. In the actual
narrative he is spoken of as one of whom God
is ashamed: "And it came to pass, when God destroyed the cities of the plain, that *God remembered
Abraham*, and sent Lot out of the midst of the
overthrow, when He overthrew the cities in the
midst of which Lot dwelt." Lot has been under
the cover, and God must use the cover toward
him. He is the God of Abraham; how could He
call Himself the God of Lot? How solemn this
treatment of one of His own! Reader, how is it
with you this moment as before God? Is He con-
fessing, or denying you? This is not a question
which you can turn off by saying, I am a Christian.
It is on that very ground that it appeals to you.

In the history, then, we find God making Himself strange to Lot. This was what His governmental ways required—the discipline that the need
of his soul called for at the time. The need past
and gone, as He looks *back* upon that history now,
He can pick out of it the good He had marked all
through, and say how precious to Him, even in a
Lot, was the trouble of soul which the iniquity of
Sodom gave him. Such is our God! such is His
holiness, and such His grace!

But then how clear this makes it that it was not
because Lot had taken part in the wickedness of
Sodom that the Lord was thus displeased! It was
simply on account of his being *there*, even as of
Abraham that tent-life of his is marked out for His
special approval: "By faith he sojourned in the
land of promise as in a strange country, dwelling
in tabernacles with Isaac and Jacob, heirs with
him of the same promise . . . . These all died
in faith, not having received the promises, but

having seen them afar off, and were persuaded of them, and embraced them, and confessed that they were strangers and pilgrims on the earth. . . . . But now they desire a better country, that is, a heavenly; wherefore God is not asnamed to be called their God; for He hath prepared for them a city." (Heb. xi. 9, 13, 16.)

Thus, then, we are right in saying that the tent at Mamre and the gate of Sodom are character-istic and contrasted things. Faith, looking for a city which hath foundations, is content to scratch the earth with a tent-pole merely. This was Abra-ham's place, pattern as he is, and father of all them that believe; and God comes to commune with him, in the broad open day—"in the heat of the day."

The style of His coming is as noticeable as all else: there is no distance, there is intimacy: it is three *men* who come; in fact, two angels, and One before whom the angels vail their faces. But they come as men, and keep this place—the more strik-ingly, because in the next chapter we find those who had left Abraham still as two men appear in Sodom explicitly as angels. Clearly, 'this differ-ence has meaning in it. How sweet a foreshadow-ing of what in due time was to take place—the tabernacling in flesh of Him in whom faith real-izes the glory of Immanuel, now no more to faith a Visitant merely.

And Abraham's practiced heart knew under all disguises Him who stood there. We learn this plainly from the first words with which he wel-comes One whom yet in this garb he has never seen before. "Lord," he says, distinguishing Him by a title only given to God, "if now I have found favor in Thy sight, pass not away, I pray Thee, from Thy servant; let a little water, I pray you, be fetched, and wash your feet, and rest yourselves under the tree: and I will fetch a morsel of bread, and comfort ye your hearts; after that ye shall pass on: for therefore are ye come unto your servant."

The faith that recognizes, entertains in the same simplicity Him whom it recognizes. There is none of the unbelieving cry so often heard, "We have seen God, and we shall die." In beautiful confidence of faith, he meets Him who has come to him as man, and as man gives Him human welcome. If He stoop to come so, he will not say, "That be far from Thee, Lord," but receive Him as He comes, putting undoubtedly before Him whatever he has, and being met with unhesitating acceptance. "He stood by them under the tree, and they did eat."

And do you, beloved reader, in the like unsuspicious way receive the grace which has now come to us in a Christ made fully known? or do you, alas! draw back from His approach, as if He knew not the full reality of the place which He has taken with us, or else the full reality of what we are, among whom He has come? I cannot find that Abraham even put his dress in order to appear before the Lord Almighty. His best and his worst were not so far apart as to make him think of it. There was no preparation of himself to appear before Him who knew him through and through. Just as he was, whatever he was, the love that met him was worthy of reception, then and there: all the sweeter and more wonderful the more he was unworthy.

But in fact, if we translate these figures, Abraham has that which may well, wherever He finds it, bring the Lord in to have communion with us. These "three measures of fine meal," and this "calf, tender and good:" do you not recognize them? Surely wherever such food is found there will still be found the Lord in company. It is Christ of whom these things speak, and occupation with Christ is still the essential and only prerequisite for communion. It is when the apostle has introduced to us, in just such nearness as was Abraham's here, that eternal life which was with the Father, and heard, seen, looked upon, and handled with the hands among us here, that he says, "That which we have seen and heard declare we unto you, that ye may have fellowship with us," and then he adds, "and truly our fellowship is with the Father, and with His Son Jesus Christ."

If, then, our souls lack fellowship,—if we are out of communion,—ought we not to ask ourselves if the great primary lack be not of occupation with Christ? Other things, no doubt, will enter in where this is absent, and we shall not be able to return to feed on Him until these things be judged and removed. But here is the first point of departure, as with Israel the turning from the manna.

Abraham's tent is provided, then, with that with which he entertains a heavenly guest. First, the three measures of meal tell of Christ personally. The "meal" is not merely this: it is the "fine flour" of the meat-offering afterward, which we all know represents Him. It is Christ as man, the Bread of life, the food of His people. But what then are the "three measures"? What is the measure of the Man Christ Jesus? Nothing less, surely, than this, that "in Him dwelleth all the

fullness of the Godhead bodily." And is not this
what the number three, the number of the Trinity
—that is, of divine fullness, speaks?* The "calf,"
on the other hand,—not necessarily what this implies for us, but a young, fresh animal—no less
clearly reminds us of Him who was the true and
perfect Workman for God. And here that mystery, which we have before seen after the flood
began to be pressed upon man, that life given up
must sustain life, is once more told out.

In Scripture thus the person and work of Christ
are kept ever together: it is not a work alone, but
a living Person who has accomplished the work.
Where we have Him before us really, communion
with God there cannot but be. How sweet that
thus, Lord's day by Lord's day at least, the bread
and the wine are to be before us, to occupy our
very hands and eyes—so busy with the things of
time and sense as they are—with Him who claims
the whole man for Himself,—that is, for fullest
joy and blessing; that afresh and afresh He in His
person and work may make communion with
God our power to go though a world which has
rejected Him.

And now Abraham is to receive the final message that the long-expected promise shall be fulfilled. Intimately connected, surely, with the scene
before us (if we look through the figure to that of
which it speaks,) is the birth of Isaac now announced. It was a "son born" that was to make
Abraham's heart glad,† and we know of whom

---

*The same exactly as in the parable in Matthew xiii. I cannot but un-
derstand, therefore, that it is Christ also that is represented there : it is
the food of God's people which the professing church, having assumed
the teacher's chair, is leavening with false doctrine.

† "Isaac" means "Laughter."

Isaac is the type. Is it not of Christ come to dwell—no more to visit merely—that the figure speaks? Thus we have here what filled the apostle's heart so afterward for the Ephesians, and bowed his knees to the Father of our Lord Jesus Christ: "That He would grant unto you, according to the riches of His glory, to be filled with might by His Spirit in the inner man; that Christ may dwell in your hearts by faith; that ye, being rooted and grounded in love, may be able to comprehend with all saints the length and depth and breadth and height; and to know the love of Christ, which passeth knowledge, that ye might be filled with all the fullness of God."

But this we shall have to look at more in another place. We have now to see as the fulfillment and fruit of communion, the Lord disclosing to Abraham the doom of Sodom, now just ready to overwhelm her. How striking are the words in which He counsels with Himself as to this, permitting us also to hear that counsel! "And the Lord said, 'Shall I hide from Abraham that thing which I do, seeing that Abraham shall surely become a great and mighty nation, and all the nations of the earth shall be blessed in him? for I know him, that he will command his children and his household after him, and they shall keep the way of the Lord, to do justice and judgment; that the Lord may bring upon Abraham all that He hath spoken of him.'"

How beautiful this testimony to one who could be called "the friend of God"! How sweet the encouragement in maintaining in one's household an authority rapidly being given up in these days—an authority from God and for God! "He will

command, . . . *and they shall* keep the way of the
Lord." Do we not see the connection also between
the man of God and the prophet? It was the constant title of these—men of God: Abraham too is
called "a prophet." "And surely," says Amos,
"the Lord God will do nothing, but He revealeth
His secret unto His servants the prophets." To
be with God is the way to penetrate the reality of
things even of the world itself. And it is in this
way that the book of Revelation addresses itself to
Christ's servants, "to show unto them the things
which must shortly come to pass."

How carefully and patiently God judges, moreover, as to Sodom,—no indifference, with all His
apparent slowness! How that full oversight and
patient judgment of every thing are affirmed!
"And the Lord said, 'Because the cry of Sodom
and Gomorrah is great, and because their sin is
very grievous; I will go down now, and see
whether they have done altogether according to
the cry of it, which is come unto Me; and if not,
I will know.'"

"And the men turned their faces from thence,
and went toward Sodom; but Abraham stood yet
before the Lord."

And now Abraham takes the place which it was
surely one part of the design of this gracious communication to put him into—the place of intercession. For us whose characters are to be formed
by the apprehension of Christ, and who know Him
now as in this very place of intercession, how important it is to realize what is before us here! It
is His people for whom the Holy Spirit intercedes
below. Abraham's prayer too follows the same
pattern: "And Abraham drew near and said, 'Wilt

Thou also destroy the righteous with the wicked?
Peradventure there be fifty righteous within the
city, wilt Thou also destroy and not spare the
place for the fifty righteous that are therein?
That be far from Thee to do after this manner, to
slay the righteous with the wicked; and that the
righteous be as the wicked, that be far from Thee:
shall not the Judge of all the earth do right?'"

How strange the implied doubt here in Abraham's mind! What poor weak questions do not
these minds of ours raise! An Abraham praying
the Judge of all the earth to do right! Is it not a
first principle that of course He must? How
could he doubt? we say. Beloved, do we never?
and how much more do we know of God than
Abraham could do possibly! How large a portion
of our prayers, if they were analyzed, would be
resolved into this, the asking God to do right!
Alas! what infidelity, even as to first principles,
cleaves to us when we little suspect it! God will
do right! Why, of course. Oh, but when every
thing on earth seems as if it were going wrong,—
when with Jacob we are tempted to say, "All these
things are against us,"—when with Job we have to
take our place upon the dust-heap, has there never
the bitter question sprung up in our hearts, if it
brake not the door of our lips,—do we never at
least have to still our hearts with it,—"Shall not
the Judge of all the earth do right?"

But it is beautiful to see how Abraham flings it
all out—doubt and all, casts it down before God.
"Pour out your hearts before Him," says the
Psalmist; "Be careful for nothing," adds the apostle; "but in every thing by prayer and supplication with thanksgiving let your requests be made

known unto God." In these very requests, what
a multitude of things unworthy of Him! but He
who has known them in the heart before would
have us pour them out in His presence, and oh the
relief that the heart gets so! How many of these
workings of unbelief do the psalms thus give us!
but they are poured out before God, and the soul
stills itself in that blessed presence as no where
else can it be stilled. What! we have been asking
God if He is God! "O thou afflicted, tossed with
tempest, and not comforted," peace! He is indeed
the "God and Father of our Lord Jesus Christ."

On the other hand, the intercession is right, and
of God. He will do all things well. He will care
for His saints whether we ask Him or not: Christ
intercedes; could we add any thing to the efficacy
of His intercession? is it not all-prevailing? does
it not cover all? Yes, yes, yes, He into whose
hands God has given His people is surely the
merciful and faithful High-Priest, never forgetting
those whom He bears upon His breast before God.
Yet none the less is it ours to pray "with all
prayer and supplication for all saints." He has
ordained, in His grace to us, that that flow of
abundant blessing which He pours out upon His
people should flow, in part at least, through chan-
nels of our own providing. He has given us fellowship with Himself in His love and care for His
people. How blessed this fellowship! Is it not,
I ask again, in a peculiar way our privilege who
are one with Him who as man has entered into
the presence of God, and with whom we are one,
surely not in position only, but in heart and spirit
also? Thus the Spirit maketh intercession for the
saints according to God; and in our hearts where

this intercession is made, if there be prayer "in the Holy Ghost," it will still be "intercession for the *saints:*" not for me or mine (in the narrow human sense), not for individual saints dear to me merely; not for sect or party; but "for all saints"! O for more power for this broad and blessed outlook, with Christ for the whole field of those that are His! O for more ability to throw ourselves in with them into their joys, their sorrows, their cares, their exercises; to "bear one another's burdens, and so fulfill the law of Christ;" to realize our oneness with Him, as we take His own into our arms and hearts in real and hearty recognition of eternal kinship!

Sodom's judgment is indeed, alas! near at hand; and little does the proud and self-sufficient world dream, (just ready to throw off openly the rule of the ordained Ruler of the scene of His rejection,) that it is the "fifty righteous" that alone have suspended divine judgment hitherto. How solemn their condition for whom presently no prayer will any more avail!

There is no rebuke with God, but a full answer. "And the Lord said, 'If I find fifty righteous within the city, then I will spare all the place for their sake.'" Abraham goes further. But it is not needful to go through the detail, so familiar as it is, of these requests which, pressed on and on, find nothing but acceptance from the patient goodness of God; until at last Abraham's faith fails, but *not* God's goodness: for we read that "it came to pass, when God destroyed the cities of the plain, that God *remembered Abraham*, and sent Lot out of the midst of the overthrow, when He overthrew the cities in the midst of which Lot dwelt."

Lot.

"AND there came two angels to Sodom at even; and Lot sat in the gate of Sodom: and Lot seeing them rose up to meet them: and he bowed himself with his face toward the ground; and he said, 'Behold now, my lords, turn in, I pray you, into your servant's house, and tarry all night, and wash your feet, and ye shall rise up early and go on your ways.' And they said, 'Nay; but we will abide in the street all night.'"

How every circumstance seems designed to bring out the contrast! Two angels come, not men: there is distance, not familiarity; and the Lord Himself does not come nigh. Hence communion there is not and cannot be. Evening, too, is fallen; they come in gloom, and as if not to be seen. And although Lot's hospitality is as ready as Abraham's, there is no such readiness in the response. They yield, however, to his urgency,—"And he pressed upon them greatly, and they turned in unto him, and entered into his house; and he made them a feast, and did bake unleavened bread, and they did eat."

But even the semblance of communion is not possible for him. Out of the path of faith, he is not master of circumstances, but they of him. The men of Sodom break in upon him, and the very attempt to entertain the heavenly guests only provokes the outbreak of the lusts of the flesh. Instead of the good he seeks, Lot has to listen to a message of judgment, which falls upon all with which he has chosen to associate himself.

How solemn is the lesson of all this in a day when heaven is indeed allowed to be the final

home of the saint, but in no wise his present practical abiding-place; when Christians count it no
shame to be citizens of this world, to be "yoked"
in every possible way—commercially, politically,
socially, and even ecclesiastically—"with unbelievers;" to sit as judges in the gate of Sodom,
and mend a scene out of which He who came in
blessing for it has been rejected, and which, when
He comes again, for that rejection, He comes to
judge! If all this be not just Lot's place, what is
it? Personal "righteousness"—in the low sense
in which necessarily we must think of it here,—
no more exempts one from the condition pictured
than it actually exempted Lot. God's Word per-
sists in claiming one's voluntary associations as
part of one's personal state. *Not* to be "unequally
yoked with unbelievers" is the condition God
gives upon which alone our Father can "*be* a
Father to us;" to be "purged" from "vessels to
dishonor" is the only state which has attached to
it the promise, "*He* shall be a vessel unto honor,
sanctified and meet for the Master's use, and prepared to every good work." (2 Cor. vi. 17, 18;
2 Tim. ii. 21.)

I am well aware that such principles are too
narrow to meet with aught but contemptuous rejection in the present day. Evangelical leaders
even can now take their places openly on public
platforms with Unitarians and skeptics of almost
every grade; and societies, secret or public, can
link together all possible beliefs in the most hearty
good fellowship. It is this that marks the time as
so near the limit of divine long-suffering, that the
very people who are orthodox as to Christ can
nevertheless be so easily content to leave Him

aside on any utilitarian plea by which they may have fellowship with His rejecters. Do they think that they can thus bribe the Father to forget His Son, or efface the ineffaceable distinction between the righteous and the wicked as "him that serveth God, and him that serveth Him not"? Alas! they can make *men* forget this, and easily teach the practical unimportance—and so, really, the untruthfulness,—of what in their creed they recognize.

O for a voice to penetrate to the consciences of God's people before judgment comes to enforce the distinction they refuse to make, and to separate them from what they cling to with such fatal pertinacity! The days of Lot are in their character linked in our Lord's words with "the day when the Son of Man is revealed." May his history, as we recount it, do its work of warning to our souls.

Communion we have found to be one thing impossible for Lot in Sodom. It is surely what is implied in that assurance on God's part,—"I will be a Father to you,"—which He conditions upon our taking the separate place from what is opposed to Him that our relationship to Him necessitates. How is it possible, indeed, if "whoever will be the friend of the world is the enemy of God," to have communion with both at the same time? How is it possible to say to the world, "I will walk with you," and stretch out the other hand to God, saying, "Walk with me"?

But if this be so, communion with God must be how rare a thing! How many things must be substituted for it, and, with the terrible self-deception which we can practice on ourselves, to be taken to be this even! With most, indeed, how little is Christ abidingly the occupation and enjoyment of the soul! And when we *would* be with Him, in our seasons of habitual or special devotion, how often do we perhaps all realize the intrusion of other thoughts,—unwelcome as, to Lot, were the men of Sodom. We are apt, at least, to console ourselves that they *are* unwelcome, perhaps to silence, or seek to silence, conscience with the thought, as if this relieved us from responsibility about them. Yet who could assert that Lot was not responsible for the intrusion of the men of Sodom? If their being unwelcome settled the whole matter, there is no doubt that they were unwelcome. But why had Abraham no such intruders?

The thoughts that throng upon us when we would gladly be free—at the Lord's table, at the prayer-meeting, or elsewhere,—have we indeed no responsibility as to these? The effort necessary to obtain what when obtained we can so little retain, while other things flock in with no effort, does it not reveal the fact of where we are permitting our hearts to settle down?

It may be, perhaps, a strange and inconsistent thing at first sight, in view of what has been already said, and if we are to find a figure here in Lot's case as in Abraham's,—that he has the materials wherewith to entertain his heavenly visitants. It is true he has neither the "calf, tender and good," which Abraham has, nor the "three measures of meal." Applying these figures, we may say that Christ is not, in the way thus pictured, present to the soul of one in Lot's case. Yet he has, what may seem almost as hard to realize, that "unleavened bread" with which the apostle bids us keep our passover-feast, and which he interprets for us as "the unleavened bread of *sincerity and truth*." How, then, may we attribute this to Lot?

The answer seems to me an exceedingly solemn one. It is found, I doubt not, in the very first case in which the command to keep the feast of unleavened bread was carried out. *How*, in fact, and why, was it carried out? Nothing would seem clearer than to say, Because the Lord enjoined it. But it is not this that Scripture itself gives as the reason.

"And the people took their dough before it was leavened; their *kneading-troughs being bound up in their clothes upon their shoulders. . . . .* And they baked unleavened cakes of the dough which they brought forth out of the land of Egypt: for it was not leavened; *because they were thrust out of Egypt, and could not tarry;* neither had they prepared for themselves any victual." (Ex. xii. 34, 39.)

That is, their obedience to the divine command was not the fruit, alas! of the *spirit* of obedience. It was the product of necessity, the fruit of their being forced out of Egypt. And do we not, indeed, easily recognize in the Church's history under what circumstances in general the feast has thus been kept? Has it not been when by the hostility of the world she has been *forced out* of the world? Persecution has always helped men to reality. If it be simply a question between open acceptance of Christ or explicit rejection of Him, this will be a matter necessarily settled alike by every Christian. The black or white would have no possible shades of intermediate gray. The "perilous times" of the last days are not such to the natural life. All the more are they perilous to the soul.

Similarly, in the shadow of calamity and distress

men wake up to reality. Their desire, the object of their lives, is taken from them, but the stars come out in the saddened sky. Face to face with eternity they have to learn how "man walketh in a vain show, and disquieteth himself" too "in vain." There are times when even Lots become real. Yet, as the mere fruit of circumstance, it has no necessary permanence in it, nor any power to lift to a higher level one in fact so low. Nay, a Lot stripped of his cover, how degraded does he seem! Strip some of my readers, perhaps, of every artificial help to make something of them,—of every thing outside the man himself,—what would be the result? Yet to this it must come: aye, to this. We brought nothing into this world; we can carry nothing out: the world passeth away and the lust thereof. If our hearts have chosen that which passes, retain it we cannot. We must some day stand where Lot stood, and hear, as he did, words of judgment from the very lips of grace.

"And the men said unto Lot, 'Hast thou here any besides? son-in-law, and thy sons, and thy daughters, and whatsoever thou hast in the city, bring them out of this place: for we will destroy this place, because the cry of them is waxen great before the face of the Lord; and the Lord hath sent us to destroy it.'"

And then we find how utter had been the wreck of testimony with a man personally righteous. Nay, that character of his (who can doubt?) would only contribute to the rejection of so strange a story as that God would visit with signal judgment for its wickedness a place so attractive as Sodom had proved to righteous Lot. God, then, it would seem, had not been in sympathy with him. This was his own confession: but if He now were, who could then possibly tell? "He seemed as one that mocked unto his sons-in-law."

Here we have, clearly, designed, sharp contrast with what had been God's own testimony as to Abraham's household. Evil has thus its law and order, we may be assured, as good has. "Train up a child in the way he should go, and when he is old he will not depart from it." Train him up for the world, and can you marvel if your work be as successful?

"And when the morning arose, then the angels hastened Lot, saying, 'Arise, take thy wife and thy two daughters which are here, lest thou be consumed in the iniquity of the city.' And while he lingered, the men "—notice how in the time of his strait the more familiar term is used again,—"the men laid hold upon his hand and the hand of his wife and the hand of his two daughters, (the Lord being merciful to him,) and they brought him forth and set him without the city."

But now the shipwreck he had made of faith begins to be apparent in him. How often do you hear people speak of not having "faith for the path"! Here, it becomes plain that what is needed is to have the *path* in order to *faith*. How, indeed, can one speak of faith except for God's path? Can we have faith to walk in some way that is not God's? or does He put before us one way for faith, and some alternative way if we will be excused from the necessity of faith?

If we have not, then, faith for the path, we must walk, manifestly, in unbelief, where God is not with us, where no promise of His assures us, where the might of His arm cannot be reckoned on. What a thing for men to choose—from weakness, as they would urge, or fear—a path in which God is not! Surely the sense of weakness it is *not* which drives men away from Him: it is willfulness, or love of the world,—sin; but never weakness.

Had one to ask really, Have I faith for the path? who could dare to say he had? This excuse might well excuse us all. Which of us knows where God's path may lead? The one thing certain is, it will be a path contrary to nature, impossible to mere flesh and blood. Had we in this sense to count the costs,—or better, to meet the charges of the way, we would all be bankrupts the first day's journey.

But is there, then, no Shepherd of the sheep? or does He not lead now in green pastures, and beside still waters? and even in the valley of death-shade is there no virtue in His rod and staff? shall we malign a path which is His path, or count upon all that which calls for His power and grace, but not upon Himself to show this?

In the path it is that He sustains the faith for the path. Out of the path, faith goes overboard at the first step; and then the after-life becomes necessarily the diligent practice of an unbelief which strengthens itself with all the maxims of sense and selfishness and worldly calculation. In Lot we have to recognize now this utter prostration of faith in a believer.

"And it came to pass, when they had brought him forth abroad, that he said, 'Escape for thy life; look not behind thee, neither stay thou in all the plain; escape to the mountain, lest thou be consumed.'

"And Lot said unto them, 'Oh, not so, my Lord;

behold now, thy servant hath found grace in thy sight, and thou hast magnified thy mercy which thou hast shown me in saving my life; and I cannot escape to the mountain, lest some evil take me, and I die: behold now, this city is near to flee unto, and it is a little one: oh, let me escape thither, (is it not a little one?) and my soul shall live!'"

How many prayers does not unbelief dictate! and how plainly does it characterize this prayer throughout! He owns a mercy he yet dare not trust; asks God for Zoar as a little city, that He might spare as such; and for his own good, not the human lives that were involved. How base is unbelief! How wonderful the goodness that, at such intercession, could spare Zoar!

But for Lot there is no revival. His wife's end follows, involved in the destruction of the city from which she had never really separated. Then he leaves Zoar, haunted still by the unbelieving fear which had taken him there at first. Finally, he is involved in the infamy of his own children, and his death is unrecorded: he had died before.

Thus far, if the anchorage be lost, may the vessel drift. And this is what the Spirit of God has put before us as the contrasted alternative with the life of faith in Abraham. Let us remember that the grossness of the outward history here may have its representative before God in what to mere human eyes may appear as correct as can be. God knoweth the heart. Blessed be His name, He has shown us also what is on His own.

The Philistines.

AFTER the judgment of Sodom, and before Isaac is yet born, we find Abraham again in the south country, and in connection with a people who in the after-history of Israel have a much more important place. Throughout the times of Samson, Eli, Samuel, and Saul, (whom they defeat and slay,) the Philistines hold the chief place among the enemies of Israel. David defeats and subjugates them, although they appear again in the times of his degenerate successors.

Their typical importance must correspond to their place in an inspired history of "things" which "happened unto them for types," and their general history and character throw light upon what is written of them in that part of Genesis to which we are now come.

The Philistines were not Canaanites, although sons of Ham. They sprang, according to Genesis x. 14, from Mizraim, to whom the land of Egypt gave its distinctive name. Yet we find them in the land of Canaan always, on the lowland of the south-west coast, with their outlook indeed toward Egypt, with which they had (as see Ex. xiii. 17,) the freest and most unobstructed communication.

To translate this spiritually, they are natural men in heavenly things. Of Ham and Mizraim we have already briefly spoken. Ham is the darkness of resisted light, and out of this, Egypt, the natural world, is come. Its name, "Mizraim," or "double straitness," applies with unmistakable clearness to the strip of land on either side of the river, maintained in fertility and beauty by its yearly overflow, and bounded strictly by the des-

ert on either hand.   From their land the people
derive their name.   As natural men, they are
conditioned and limited between narrow bounds,
within which they may do great things, but not
transcend them.   They are governed and charac-
terized by their conditions, naturally; are governed and get their name from what they should
govern.

Such limits—indeed, much narrower,—confine
the Philistines to their strip of sea-coast.   They
hold but a border of the land; and, however fertile,
its lowest part.   Other parts they may ravage, not
really possess: there, they are (according to their
name) "wanderers" merely.   Here too they are
sojourners in a land that is not theirs: it belongs
already, in divine purpose, to the seed of that
"Abram the Hebrew," who now comes to Gerar,
no wanderer, but a "passenger," or pilgrim.   To
the one alone is there a future, a fixed point beyond, faith in him the substance of things hoped
for, the evidence of things not seen.   Yet as the
order is, first, that which is natural, and afterward
that which is spiritual, the Philistines for long
seem to possess the land.   Abraham already finds a
king at Gerar whose name, however interpreted,*
speaks of established, successional authority, while
the captain of his host is Phichol—*i. e.*, the "voice
of all."   Who that is prepared to find meaning
here at all can fail to see in this the shadow of that
traditional authority to which human religiousness, ignorant of the living Spirit, ever appeals?
And completely in accordance with this it is that
with Abraham and Isaac, as with the men of faith
of every age, their great contention is about the

---

*Abimelech: either "Father of a king," or "Whose father [is] king."

wells of water which they themselves never dig, but of which they would with violence possess themselves, only to stop them again with earth. Of how many Sitnahs and Eseks has church-history been the record, until in God's mercy a Rehoboth came and they who sought the truth found "room"! All this in its general meaning seems easy enough to follow, and to make the typical character of these Philistines very clear.

It is noteworthy, too, that while never themselves possessing more than a border of it, they have loomed so largely in men's eyes as to give their name to the whole land. *Pa*lestine is only *Phi*lestine. So the traditional church is "catholic" —universal.

And now at Gerar we find Abraham once more failing as long before he had failed in Egypt. These Philistines, too, are but Egyptians, though in Canaan; even as the world, though come into the church, is still the world. Sarah, the covenant of grace, belongs still and only to the man of faith; but how often has he failed to assert this absolutely exclusive claim! In the present day there is surely more failure in this respect than ever; when, with an open Bible ours, and more enlightenment, Protestant traditions are become the rule of what is no less a world-church than Rome itself. For such, the Abimelechs and Phichols will have their place as of old; human authority be substituted for divine; the wells which faith had dug be stopped again. And here, how great the danger of Sarah being given up,—of grace being divorced from faith!

Alas! the liberality of the day is gone so far in this direction, that grace must not be denied where

not only faith, but *the* faith, is absent,—where
Christ is Himself denied.   Orthodox and unortho-
dox mingle on platform and in pulpit.   All lines
are being surely and not slowly effaced.   Churches
with orthodox creeds open their doors widely to
whatever is popular enough to make it worth their
while; and Christians, with whatever trouble of
conscience or grief of heart, dare not purge themselves from the evils which they feebly lament.
They have obeyed one scriptural injunction at
least,—they have "counted the cost:" alas! with
too cold a calculation, into which neither the glory
of God nor even their own true blessing has been
allowed to come.

How little man's hand is competent to hold what
God has intrusted to it we may see in Abraham.
It is not the young and raw disciple, but the man
who has walked in the path of faith for long, who
here shows himself ready to give up the partner
of his life, and the depositary of all the promises!
What then is man? and what hope for him except
in God?   None, surely.   And it is to ground us
well in this that we are given to see the sad and
terrible failure of these honored servants of God.
Not to discourage, but to lead us to the source
of all confidence and strength.   Only in realized
weakness do we find this.   Only when unable to
do without God for a moment do we find what
He is for us moment by moment.

And it is the best blessing that we show most
our incompetence to hold.   Our place in Christ is
that upon which all else for us depends, yet who
of those to whom God has in His goodness been
showing it in these last days is not aware how the
knowledge of it had for ages almost disappeared

out of the faith of Christians? Justification by
faith, given similarly back to us in Reformation
days, has been only by the same goodness preserved by constant revivals out of perpetual
decline since then. Well for us will it be in
proportion as we learn these lessons and our faith
takes hold upon the living God. Alas! that even
here the very failure of man should tend to shake
our hold of *His* faithfulness,—as if *He*, not we, had
failed! But "hearken unto Me, O house of Jacob,
and all the remnant of the house of Israel, which
are borne by Me from the belly, which are carried
from the womb, even to your old age, I am He;
even to hoar hairs will I carry you: I have
made, and I will bear; even I will carry, and
will deliver you."

In a marked way God interferes here for His
failing servant, suffering him indeed to find for
awhile the fruit of his own ways, but coming in
for him at last in how tender and gracious a manner, to speak of him as "a prophet," and to make
Abimelech debtor to his prayers. How different
from our own ways with one another, ready as we
are so easily to give up each other, sometimes at
the mere suspicion of wrong-doing, when faith
would hold fast the people of God for God!
How sweet and restoring too for Abraham's soul
this goodness of the ever-faithful One! for grace
it is that restores alone: "sin shall not have
dominion over you, because ye are not under
law, but under grace."

Let us hold each other fast for God, if of this
grace indeed we would be ministers. Members of
Christ as we are, we are members also, and thus,
of one another. This bond will survive all failure,

and it should in whatever failure be felt (the more, not the less, for the strain upon it,) in our hearts.

And now, unmoved from His own purposes of wisdom and of love, the Lord fulfills to Abraham the promise that He had made. A son is given to gladden his life, and be the pledge of mercies still to come. Isaac is born, type of a greater, in whom all promises find completion. In Him, dwelling in the heart by faith, the life of faith finds its completion. From the first its one necessity, He now becomes its abiding realization. Let us look at this briefly, as the prayer in Ephesians iii. develops it.

The apostle's prayer is to "the Father of our Lord Jesus Christ, of whom *every** family in heaven and earth is named." Christ in His place as Man, yet Son of the Father, is a new link of relationship between God and all His creatures. Angels as well as men have their place here. It is impossible but that the place He takes must affect all. He is Head over all things, as well as Head to His body the Church: the "First-born of every creature,"—"Beginning of the creation of God." The arms which reach to man at the farthest distance encompass all between. The love which has displayed itself toward the lowest is felt as a pulse of new life by every rank of the unfallen "sons of God." Every family of these has for its Father the Father of our Lord Jesus Christ. How this at once sets the one in whose heart by faith Christ dwells at the centre of all the divine purposes! How "length and breadth and depth and height" begin to dawn upon him whose eye rests upon Him by whom and for whom all things were

---

* So, rightly, the Revised Version, with Alford, Ellicott, etc.

created! No wonder, therefore, that the apostle prays "that He would grant unto you, *according to the riches of His glory*, to be strengthened with might by His Spirit in the inner man, that Christ may dwell in your hearts by faith." The "inner man" and the "heart" are parallel in meaning in Scripture: the "*hidden* man of the heart," as Peter calls it; not affections merely, but the whole man himself—the true man under all appearances. Here, in the centre and citadel of his being, faith receives its Lord.

Christ dwelling in the heart by faith redeems us then from the narrowness and pettiness of mere individual interests, and brings us into the plans and counsels of a wisdom that embraces all things. "Rooted and grounded" ourselves "in love," which has met and satisfied all need in so wondrous a manner, "breadth and length and depth and height" begin to be revealed to us. All mysteries find solution in the deeper mystery of the cross. Evil is no where else so evil, but it is no where else so met, defeated, triumphed over, by the inherent power of good. And it is good which is in God Himself toward us, which manifests and glorifies Him.

The "breadth and length and depth and height," of which the apostle speaks, are not, of course, measures of "the love of Christ, which," he declares, "passeth knowledge;" yet are they the means of better knowing how infinite it is. The "love" in which we are "rooted and grounded" alone enables us to "comprehend the breadth and length and depth and height;" and these apprehended, heaven and earth, time and eternity, are filled forthwith with the fullness of a divine presence.   We know the love of Christ, which passeth knowledge, and are filled up in all the fullness of God.

This is the consummation of the life of faith when the true Isaac dwells thus with us.   It is the conclusion, therefore, of this section of the book before us, save only the brief appendix in which we see, first, the bondwoman and her child cast out, and then the Philistines owning the superiority of the pilgrim man of faith.

The first has a dispensational application, which the apostle gives us in Galatians iv; and here Isaac appears, not as the representative of Christ Himself, but of those who by grace are one with Him.   "Now we, brethren, as Isaac was, are the children of promise; but as then he that was born after the flesh persecuted him that was born after the Spirit, even so it is now.   Nevertheless what saith the Scripture?   'Cast out the bondwoman and her son; for the son of the bondwoman shall not be heir with the son of the freewoman.'"

In Christianity God had for the first time recognized relationship with a family not born after the flesh, as in Judaism Israel as a nation was, but with those spiritually born of Him.   The children of law were born to bondage; the children of grace alone are free.   But the Church had, as Isaac, its weaning-time, before the child of the bondwoman was cast off.   The larger part of the Acts illustrates this, which the close of the fifth of Hebrews explains and applies.   The last chapter of this epistle shows the camp rejected,—Ishmael and Hagar, the nation on the footing of the legal covenant.

Cast out, they wander in the wilderness of Beersheba, and are nigh perishing for thirst. This I conceive to be the present condition of Israel. The water, the word of life, is spent for them, and the well they see not, although the oath of God, the covenant with their fathers, secures it for their final possession.* This, therefore, their eyes shall yet be opened to, and Hagar herself become a means of blessing to them (Deut. xxx. 1–3.); their dwelling still and ever outside of Canaan—the heavenly inheritance.

The development of these things would be full of interest, but would lead us too far to follow. The individual application is clear in general, although the details may be less easy to trace. Most interesting is it to see that the Philistine has now to concede that "God is with" the man of faith, and that the well of water is all his own. Here, then, afresh he worships, calling on Jehovah, the everlasting God.

---

* "Beersheba" means "The well of the oath." (Ver. 14.)

Sec. 5.—*Isaac.* (*Chap. xxii–xxvi.* 33.)

(1.) *The Dispensational Application.*—In the chapter to which we are now come, the outward application has a prominence which it scarcely has elsewhere in the book of Genesis. No wonder, since in Isaac we have Christ personally, the central theme of the Spirit of God. The lapse here of that individual application which we have found so continuous hitherto,—the thread, indeed, on which the other truths are strung,—has its own significance and beauty. Of course it may be said that it is difficult to say whether this lapse be more than one in our knowledge; and indeed we have no plummet to fathom the depth of our ignorance. "If any one think that he knoweth any thing, he knoweth nothing yet as he ought to know." Still the fullness of detail on the one side, so coinciding with the apparent failure on the other, seems to speak plainly. It is (if I may venture to say so,) as when the geologist finds a sudden upburst from beneath disturb the regularity of the strata he is tracing out, but finds in it the outcropping of seams of precious metal or mineral, thus exposed for man's behoof and need. It is no disturbance really of the divine plan—no interruption to that continual thought and care for us which the individual application argues. What untold blessing in being thus permitted, in fellowship with Him whose record this is, to occupy ourselves with Christ!

Is there not a lack of ability generally for this, in spite of the way in which God is opening His Word to us, that speaks sorrowfully for the state of our souls? Are not Christians dwelling upon that which they count of profit to *them*, to the

losing sight very much of that which is of greatest
profit? Is not even the gospel preached without
the witness of that box of ointment for the head of
Christ which He said should be told every where
"for a memorial [not of Him, but] of *her*"?

Isaac is undoubtedly the living type of Christ
which gives Him to us most in the work He has
done for God, and thus for us. For a moment, as
it were, from the solemn institution of sacrifice the
vail is almost removed. Man for man it is must
suffer: man, but not *this* man. Isaac is withdrawn,
and faith is left looking onward to the Lamb that
"God will provide for Himself" as a burnt-offering.

But if Isaac be the type of this, another comes no
less distinctly into view. It is a father here who
gives his son. Abraham seems, indeed, the most
prominent figure, and necessarily for the type. It
is the father's will to which the son obediently
gives himself. In the antitype, the God who pro-
vides Himself the lamb answers to the father in
this case. It is the Son of God who comes to do the
Father's will. But what a will, to be the Father's!

"And it came to pass after these things"—the
break is plain with what had gone before,—"that
God did tempt [or "try"] Abraham, and said unto
him, 'Abraham:' and he said, 'Here am I.'"

We wonder at this strange testing of a faith God
held precious. Was it not worth the while to be
honored with such a history? This was his justification by works now, God bringing out into open
sight before others that which He Himself had
long before seen and borne witness of. And then
how wonderful to see in this display of a human
heart the manifestation of the Father's!

How all is measured out to Abraham!—"And

He said, 'Take now thy son,—thine *only* son,—
Isaac,—whom thou lovest; and get thee into the
land of Moriah; and offer him there for a burnt-
offering upon one of the mountains which I will
tell thee of.'" But who can fail to see that in these
elements of sorrow that filled to the brim the father's cup we have the lineaments of a sacrifice
transcending this immeasurably? Let us not fear
to make God too human in thus apprehending
Him. He has become a man to be apprehended.

"Thy son, thine only son," God says to Abra-
ham: and "God so loved the world that He gave
His only begotten Son, that whosoever believeth
on Him should not perish, but have eternal life."
Thus is manifested His love, that it is His Son that
He has given,—His only begotten Son. This is
too human a term for some, who would fain do
Him honor by denying this to be His divine title.
They own Him Son of God, as "that holy thing"
born of the virgin Mary; they own Him too as
"God over all blessed forever;" but His *eternal*
sonship they do not own.* But thus it would not
be true that "the Father *sent the Son* to be the pro-
pitiation for our sins," nor that "God *gave* His only
begotten Son." And this term, "*only* begotten," is
in contrast with His title as "*First*-begotten,"—
"First-born among many brethren." The former
as decisively excludes others from sharing with
Him as the latter admits. And when the "Word
was made flesh, and *tabernacled* among us" (Jno. i.
14, *Gr.*), the glory of Deity seen in the tabernacle
of His manhood was "the glory as of the Only Begotten of the Father, full of grace and truth."

---

*Two popular commentaries, those of Adam Clarke and Albert Barnes,
are infected with this doctrine.

Again, if God only could fully declare God, it is "the only begotten Son, who is in the bosom of the Father, *He* hath declared Him."

John thus, whose peculiar theme is the divine manifestation in the Word made flesh, dwells upon this term, "the only begotten." "Had the Father no 'bosom,'" it has been well asked, "before Christ was born on earth?" Nay, if there were no Son before then, there was of necessity no Father either. "He that denieth the Son, the same hath not the Father."

The Jews even understood that in claiming God to be His Father, He made Himself equal with God. Men argue from it now to show that, if true in the fullest way, it would make Him inferior! No doubt one may fail, on the other hand, by insisting too much on the analogy of the merely human relationship. We are safe, and only safe, in adhering to Scripture; and there the revelation of the Father and the Son are of the essence of Christianity.

"He spared not His own Son, but delivered Him up for us all." Here we are apt to fail, not in overestimate of the Son's sacrifice, but in losing sight of the Father's. It is this surely that in these words the apostle insists on: it is this which peculiarly the type before us dwells on. Let us not miss by any thought of impassivity in God the comfort for our hearts that we should find in this. We may easily make Him hard where we would only make Him changeless. But what to us does it imply, this very title, "Father"? and who is the Author of this fount of gushing feeling within us, which if it were absent we should necessarily regard as the gravest moral defect? "He that

planted the ear, shall He not hear? He that formed
the eye, shall He not see?" and He who gave man
the tender response of the heart to every appeal of
sorrow, what must He be who has made us thus?

God has given His Son, and His heart has been
declared to us once for all. If He try us too, as
He tried Abraham, how blessed to think that in
this carefully measured cup of his, God was saying, as it were, "I know—I know it all: it is My
Son, My Isaac, My only one, I am giving for
men." The tree is cast into these Mara-waters
thus that sweetens all their bitterness.

Isaac's own submission is perfect and beautiful.
He was not the child that he is often pictured, but,
as it would appear, in the vigor of early manhood.
He nevertheless submits himself absolutely. How
fitting a type of Him who stops the resistance of
His impulsive follower with the words, "Put up
again thy sword into its sheath: the cup which
My Father hath given Me, shall I not drink it?"

Through all this trial of Abraham's we must not
miss the fact that the faith of resurrection cheers
the father's heart. The promises of God were
assured in him, of whom He had said, "In Isaac
shall thy seed be called." If therefore God called
for him to be offered up, resurrection must restore
him from the very flames of the altar; and "in a
figure," as the apostle says, from the dead he was
received. The figure of resurrection here it is very
important to keep in mind, for it is to Christ in resurrection that the events following typically refer.

In fact, Isaac is spared from death; and here
occurs one of those double figures by which the
Spirit of God would remedy the necessary defect
of all figures to set forth Christ and His work.

Isaac is spared; but there is substituted for him
"a ram caught in a thicket by his horns." Picture
of devoted self-surrender, as we have seen elsewhere the ram is; he is "caught by his horns"—
the sign (as others have noticed) of his power.
Grace recognizes our impotence as claim upon
His might: as He says, "I looked, and there was
none to help, and I wondered that there was none
to uphold; therefore Mine own arm brought salvation to Me."

In a figure, however, Isaac is raised from the
dead; and as risen, the promise is confirmed to
him,—"In thy seed shall all the nations of the
earth be blessed." It is Christ raised from the
dead who is the only source of blessing to the
whole world. The value and necessity of His
sacrificial work are here affirmed. Death has
passed upon all men, for that all have sinned; only
beyond death, then, can there be fulfillment of the
promise, however free.

With the typical meaning of what follows (in ch.
xxiii. and xxiv.) many are happily familiar now.
Sarah passes away and gives place to Rebekah,—
the mother to the bride (xxiv. 67). Sarah is here
the covenant of grace in connection with the people "of whom, as concerning the flesh, Christ
came." God's dealings with the nation, in view of
this, (for the present,) end, and a new thing is developed,—the Father's purpose to have a bride for
His risen Son. The servant's mission shows us the
coming of the Holy Ghost to effect this. Isaac
remains in Canaan, as Christ in heaven. The
Spirit of God, having all the fullness of the divine
treasury "under His hand," comes down in serv-
ant-guise as the Son came before. Thorough de-

votedness to the father's will and the son's interests
marks the servant's course. For those who are by
grace allowed to be identified with the blessed
service thus pictured, how instructive the fact that
even his name we have no knowledge of. From
what Abraham says, in chapter xv, of the steward
of his house, it is generally inferred that it is Eliezer of Damascus, but this is by no means certain.
Certainly he is the representative of One who does
not speak of Himself, or seek His own glory; and
for those whom He may use as His instruments,
the lesson is plain.

So also is that of the waiting upon God which is
so striking in Abraham's messenger. What sustains in prayer like singleness of eye? If it is our
own will we are seeking, what confidence can we
have? Here we find prayer that God answers to
the letter. If Christ's interests be ours, how fully
may we count upon God glorifying His beloved
Son! "Let it be she whom Thou hast *appointed*
for Thy servant Isaac." How blessed to be working on to an already predestined end!

As for Rebekah, it is to be noted that she is
already of Abraham's kindred: it is not an outside
stranger that is sought for Isaac; and this is surely
impressed on us in chapter xxii, where Nahor's
children are announced to Abraham. It is in the
family of faith that the Church is found: it is the
gathering together of the *children of God* who
are scattered abroad (Jno. xi. 52); not, as so many
imagine, identical with the whole company of
these, but only with those of the present period—
from Pentecost till the Lord calls up His own.
"Thou shalt go to my land and to my kindred,
and take a wife for my son Isaac." Rebekah does

not, therefore, I believe, represent the call of sinners by the gospel, but the call of saints to a place of special relationship with Christ on high. This is what began at Pentecost, plainly, where the hundred and twenty gathered were already of the "kindred;" and this is the character of the work ever since, although all that are saved now are added to the church. But this is a special grace none the less. We are in the mission-time of Genesis xxiv, and the Spirit of God is seeking a bride for the risen Son.

It is thus also, I doubt not, that Rebekah is found by the well of water, the constant figure of truth as a living reality for the soul. Already she has this, when the call is received to be Isaac's bride in Canaan. Indeed Isaac's gifts are already upon her before she receives this. She is betrothed, as it were, before she realizes or has received the message. So at Pentecost, and for years after, the Church, already begun, knew not the character of what had begun. It is only through Paul's ministry that her place with Christ is fully at last made known.

Simplicity of faith is found in Rebekah ; she believes the report of him whom she has not seen, and as the messenger will have no delay, so she on her part seeks none. The precious things she has received are earnest already of what awaits her. Details of the journey there are none; but at the end, Isaac comes to meet her. "And Rebekah lifted up her eyes, and when she saw Isaac, she lighted off the camel. For she had said unto the servant, 'What man is this that walketh in the fields to meet us?' And the servant had said, 'It is my master.' Therefore she took a vail and covered herself."

What a word for heart and conscience in all this! Are we thus simple in faith, thus prompt and unlagging? And at the end of our journey nearly now, when the cry has already gone forth, "Behold the Bridegroom!" for those to whom the Interpreter-Spirit has spoken,—shall there not be with us any thing that answers to this beautiful action of Rebekah's, when "she lighted off the camel" and "took a vail and covered herself"? It is He whose glory Isaiah saw, before whom the seraphim cover themselves; and the nearness of the place to which we are called, and the intimacy already ours, if we enjoy it, will only manifest themselves in deeper and more self-abasing reverence.

The rest is Isaac's joy. What gladness to think of *His* who even in glory waits as a Nazarite yet, to drink the wine new with us in His Father's kingdom!

In chapter xxv. we find another wife of Abraham, and a hint of the *multiplied* seed which was to be his; from which Isaac, as the heir of the promises, is separated entirely. Ishmael's family is then rehearsed. These three,—Isaac and his bride, Ishmael, and Keturah's sons,—seem sufficiently to point out the diverse blessing of the family of faith in the Church, Israel, and the millennial nations.

Further than this, whether the dispensational application can be traced, I am not clear. It is plainly a history of failure that begins, very distinct in character from the previous one; which, moreover, seems to have a very plain end in chapter xxv. 18.

(2.) *The Individual Application.*—We now come to the individual application. And here the apostle's words in the epistle to the Galatians are precise enough,—"We, brethren, as Isaac was, are the children of promise. . . . . We are not children of the bondwoman, but of the free." As Ishmael represents the child of law then, so does Isaac represent the child of grace. And this, as he has shown us in the beginning of the same chapter, is not merely the true child, but the child in the child's place It is simple that he who stands on the one hand for the Son of God should on the other represent the sons of God. It is sonship, then, that is presented to us in Isaac,—the place of the child.

In contrast with Ishmael, we find one born by divine power, not natural strength,—of grace, not law. His name, "Laughter," speaks of the father's joy in him,—for us, how precious a thought, the *Father's* joy! Our joy in such a place we naturally think of, and it may well be great; but how much greater, and how it deepens ours as we apprehend it, the Father's joy! The different interpretations of the parable of the pearl are in similar contrast. Who can wonder at the thought that a pearl of great price, precious enough to be bought with the surrender of all one has, must needs be Christ? But what a revelation to the soul that finds that under this strong figure is conveyed Christ's love for His Church! Thus Scripture, in its own unapproachable way, puts the arms of divine love about us.

How striking too is the fact of Isaac's persistent dwelling in Canaan in this connection! Abraham is found outside, and Jacob for many years, while

while Joseph spends most of his life outside: Isaac, of all of them, is the only one who is never found any where but in the land of Canaan. If it be a question of a wife of his kindred, still he must not leave to seek her; when he is in the Philistines' land, and thus on the border, God interferes by a vision, and says, "Go not down into Egypt; dwell in the land which I tell thee of; sojourn in this land, and I will bless thee." And to us, surely, the Church of the first-born ones, whom first of all among men God has claimed for Himself, the land in which we are to abide is marked out with all possible distinctness: we are claimed by Heaven, destined for the Father's house; and when re-vealed with Christ in the glory of heaven, then shall be the "manifestation of the sons of God." Meanwhile it is for us to remember the words to us so full both of warning and encouragement, "Go not down into Egypt; . . . sojourn in *this* land, and I will bless thee."

Isaac's life is indeed full of blessing, with little incident, a striking contrast to Jacob and his vary-ing experiences; he sows and reaps, and digs his wells of water in a security little disturbed. He is thus the fitting type of the child of God abiding in the serene enjoyment of his unchanging portion. This is the real Beulah of Bunyan's allegory, "where the sun shines and the birds sing day and night;" or, as Scripture better says, "a land which the Lord thy God careth for; the eyes of the Lord thy God are always upon it." Bunyan's land, however, is at the close of his pilgrim's course; and there indeed it is too often found, if found at all. But it would be a sad mistake to suppose that one must wait till then to find it. Blessed be God, it is not so: the joy of our place with God is ours by indefeasible title, and cannot be lost, save by our own connivance. God's word for us all is, "Sojourn in this land, and I will bless thee."

Yet peaceful and full of blessing as is this life of Isaac, the entrance to all its blessedness is found by a narrow door-way of exquisite trial. Isaac's sacrifice is the true beginning of his history, and the key to all that follows. This we have seen when regarding him as the undoubted type of the Son of God. It is the self-surrender of the cross which explains all that after-history. And if here, at first sight, the application to us might seem to fail, it is only to a very superficial glance. Nay, the precise aspect of the cross here is such as to bring out the lesson for us in the most striking and beautiful manner. It is as self-surrender into a Father's hands that it is presented in the type we have been considering; and seen in this way, not only is there no difficulty in the application, but the whole becomes at once a vivid picture of significant and fruitful beauty.

"I beseech you therefore, brethren," says the apostle, "by the mercies of God, that ye present your bodies a living sacrifice, holy, acceptable unto God, which is your intelligent service. And be not conformed to this world, but be ye transformed by the renewing of your mind, that ye may prove what is that good and acceptable and perfect will of God." (Rom. xii. 1, 2.) How admirably this expresses the meaning of the type before us! It is a sacrifice, a living sacrifice, we are called to,—a sacrifice in life, although as such it speaks of death:—how clearly Isaac's presents this thought to us! Here, what might seem a difficulty in the larger application becomes a special beauty in the individual one. Isaac, given up to death, does not really die. In will and intent he does; in fact, it is his substitute. So Israel, at an after-time, coming to pass through Jordan to the land of their inheritance, find Jordan all dried up, and a broad way made over its former bed. There is no need to interpret. Death in the reality of it we do not know: we do not die, but are dead, with Him who is "resurrection and life" to us. The sorrow, the bitterness, the sting, of death was His who is now, as the consequence of it, in the glory of God for us; but by virtue of it, our position is changed; our place is no more in the world; we belong to Him and to heaven, where He has gone for us. On the one side of it, this is in fact our salvation, our perfect blessing, our highest privilege; but it involves, on the other, the living sacrifice of our bodies, of that which links us with the world out of which we have passed. Alas! that we should have to speak of this as trial, but this is surely what all sacrifice implies, and "sacrifice" the apostle calls it. But it is a living sacrifice—a sacrifice, not in death, but life,—a holy offering, acceptable to God,—a surrender to Him, in which we prove what is His good and acceptable and perfect will. Trial there may be here, to such as we are; but to faith, only unspeakable privilege— the entrance upon a path which is perfect freedom. "God forbid that I should glory," says the apostle, "save in the cross of our Lord Jesus Christ, by whom the world is crucified unto me and I unto the world."

Do you understand this, beloved reader? can you appropriate so strong and triumphant an ex-

pression?   To glory in that which puts away
one's sins is easy, and it is the cross which does
this; but the apostle is not speaking of glorying in
that which puts away his sins, but in that which cru-
cifies him to the world and the world to him! The
joy which he manifests here is that alone which
gives power for the path we are considering,—
alone makes it really practicable. Joy is an essential element of the spirit in which alone God's
path can be trodden. It is a Father's will to which
we are called to surrender ourselves,—the will of
One who alone has title to have one; His will by
which we have been "sanctified through the offering of the body of Jesus Christ;" a self-surrender
into a Father's hand, to whom we are far, far more
than Isaac was to Abraham!

And yet, indeed, there is trial and sorrow in this
path, as upon what path that man's feet have ever
trodden is there not? Can the world give you one
upon which it can insure you freedom from suffering for a moment? Do the "lust of the flesh, and
the lust of the eyes, and the pride of life" promise
more to you? and can you trust its promises better
than those "exceeding great and precious ones by
which we are made partakers of the divine nature,
having *escaped* the corruption that is in the world
through lust"? No; if you be Christ's, you know
you cannot. But then, beloved, if this be your
decision, (and the Lord seeks deliberate, "intelligent" service,) let it be whole-hearted, and unwa-
veringly maintained. Surrender must be real:
there must not be limitation and reserve. If God
be worthy of trust, He is worthy of *full* trust; and
full trust means full surrender,—nothing short!

Alas! it is the foxes, "the little foxes, that spoil

the vines." It is the little compromises that destroy the vigor and freshness and reality of Christian life. It must be so, unless God could connive at His own dishonor. There is no such reserve with Isaac. He yields himself implicitly into his father's hand and will; and bitter as the cup presented to him may be, in result it is to find life in the place of death, and all the promises con- firmed to him. For us, if in the world, there must be tribulation; not only is this the appointed way to the glory already revealed to faith, but even now we may with the apostle "glory in trib- ulation also, because tribulation worketh patience, and patience experience, and experience hope, and hope maketh not ashamed, because the love of God is shed abroad in our hearts by the Holy Ghost, which is given unto us."

Thus Isaac's offering has the most pregnant meaning with reference to his after-life. In the two following chapters, the individual application seems to fail, and give place to the dispensational, as I have already remarked, although on the other hand it may be mere dimness of spiritual sight which cannot find it. Rebekah should at least have some significance here, and her taking her place in Sarah's tent seems to identify her as a form of that principle of grace which there can be no question Sarah represents. Her name also, "binding," seems in this way to add to the idea of grace that of assured perpetuity, as having found its justifying and abiding ground. Rebekah would remind us thus of that which the apostle tells us— that God hath "accepted us [the word is literally "graced"] in the Beloved." How this suits with the typical teaching of Isaac's life is plain enough,

—sonship implying, surely, the perpetuity here spoken of.

"And it came to pass, after the death of Abraham, that God blessed his son Isaac, and he dwelt by the well Lahairoi." These dwelling-places are certainly characteristic and distinctive, as Abraham's at Hebron, and Lot's in the valley of Jordan or at Sodom. A well, too, was a natural and suitable accompaniment for the tent of a pilgrim: water is a first necessity for the maintenance of life, and so is for us the "living water"—the Spirit acting through the Word. "The words that I speak unto you," says the Lord, "they are spirit and they are life."

The way that water ministers to life and growth is indeed a beautiful type of the Spirit's action. Without water, a plant will die in the midst of abundance of food in actual contact with its roots. Its office is to make food to be assimilated by the organism, and to give power to the system itself to take it up. Although the word may sometimes be otherwise used, yet in Proverbs v. 15 the *well* is distinct from the cistern as the place of "running," or "living," water. Such wells were those that Isaac digged, not mere artificial cisterns, as we find in chapter xxvi, "And Isaac's servants digged in the valley, and found there a well of springing water." Such wells should not all the children of God covet to dwell by? where not only our energy is manifest, but much more—the energy of the Spirit of God. Our diligence depending absolutely on God for its success, but where nevertheless He meets without fail the heartfelt diligence that craves for its urgent need the living water. May not and should not every one of God's Isaacs be, in his measure

and way, a well-digger? What blessedness for
him who has thus not simply the ministry of
others, but his own springing well!

Isaac's well, where above all he loved to be, was
this Lahairoi—the well that told to him, as once it
had done to Hagar, of the gracious superintending
care of an ever-living, ever-present God. What a
world is this where sin has made Him a stranger,
—which has made it necessary to seek God at all!
How much stranger still a world that can do without Him! For the heart convinced of the desolation of His absence, what cry like that for the
living God? Sonship in Isaac speaks to us here
of this cry answered and the heart's home found.
And the very essence of Christianity is in this,
that we are acknowledged sons.

To the realization of this living presence the
Word is ever necessary. The word of God is
that which (by the power of the Spirit) reveals to
us the presence of God; and thus the apostle in
the epistle to the Hebrews links the two together:
"For the word of God is quick and powerful, and
sharper than any two-edged sword, piercing even
to the dividing asunder of soul and spirit, and of
the joints and marrow, and is a discerner of the
thoughts and intents of the heart; *neither is there
any creature that is not manifest in His sight;* but
all things are naked and opened unto the eyes of
Him with whom we have to do." This, it is true,
may seem to speak more of our manifestation than
of His; but the one is the effect of the other, and
how important it is to remember this! An exercised conscience and habitual self-judgment will
be the sure results of a true walk with God. A
profession of intimacy where laxity assumes the

name of grace is the worst deception and dishonor
to God's blessed name.

And now we find with Rebekah, as with Sarah,
that fruitfulness cannot be according to nature, or
by its power. Grace as a principle implies dependence and intervention of the power of God. More
than this, that which is first is natural,—Esau is
rejected and the younger is taken up (though himself no better) in the sovereignty of God alone.

Striking it is that Isaac's history ends (for in
chapter xxvii. it is rather Jacob,) with a scene in
the Philistines' land, the similarity of which, too, to
that in Abraham's life must be plain to the dullest
reader. The repetition of the lesson gives it em-
phasis, of course. The sin here must be one of
special importance, and to which the believer must
be specially prone, to be thus emphasized. We
cannot but remember that these Philistines are
the great enemies of Israel at an after-period, and
that the history of the Judges ends really, leaving
them captive to these. If we take Scripture,—the
announcement of the sure word of prophecy, and
remember the meaning which attaches to this
Philistine power, is it not a decisive confirmation
of the truth of the interpretation already given?
For the history of the outward church does assuredly end in the prevalence of that worldly successional power which in our days is again with so
much energy asserting itself. Into this it is not
now the place to go; but prophecy is not for us
the mere prediction of the future, but the warning
for the present: we are taught to judge now be-
forehand what is then to meet God's judgment,
and here Isaac's failure and Isaac's final superiority are alike instructive.

First, let us note that the Philistine's *land* is part of God's land for Isaac, but that it is famine drives him there, which recalls, and is meant to recall, that in Abraham's time which drove him down to Egypt. God interposes to prevent Isaac also going down there: "And the Lord appeared unto him, and said, 'Go not down into Egypt; dwell in the land which I will tell thee of; sojourn in *this* land"—not necessarily or merely the Philistines'—"and I will be with thee and bless thee; for unto thee and unto thy seed will I give all these countries; and I will perform the oath which I sware unto Abraham thy father; and I will make thy seed to multiply as the stars of heaven, and will give unto thy seed all these countries.'"

The Philistines' land, then, is included in this ground. It is part of the land, yet only the outside border toward Egypt, with the corresponding danger as a dwelling-place for the man of faith. This low border-land alone, as I have before remarked, could the Philistines *occupy*, although they might make their power felt far beyond. It will be evident the line of things we have to do with here, and that it is as we approach to this border-land of external truths that we reach the place where the traditional church has built her strongholds. She can parade her ceremonies and proclaim her mysteries, and make out the land to be her own; yet it is a land in which an Abraham may dig and an Isaac re-dig many a well of living water which the would-be possessors of it treat as the sign of a hostile claim, and contend for but to stop with earth. How effectually for ages did they do this! How much have the men of faith yielded for peace's sake, as did Isaac here, until God gave them a Rehoboth. Indeed this is a ground noted for the yielding of timid saints.

The practical title to the land is the possession of the well. With it you may still find wonderful harvests, for it is a place of abundant fertility. In the region of outward things, if we have diligence to dig beneath the surface, we may find the sweet-est refreshment and the fullest satisfaction, and may sow and reap a hundredfold. Here Isaac gained his riches and became great, for the Lord blessed him. And what is Judaism?—what is the Old Testament, but such a country as this Philistines' land, where men, seeing nothing but the letter, and misinterpreting that, have built up once more a system of carnal ordinances, darkening with shadows long since done away the blessed light which has visited them? And yet in this Philistines' land, which is Israel's really, (and which God's Israel has always been so slow to claim,) how much awaits an Isaac's diligence and care, to repay them with untold riches!

This final scene in Isaac's history closes with his altar at Beersheba, and with the acknowledgment, even by the Philistines themselves, that Jehovah is with the man of faith. To the angel of the church of Philadelphia saith the Lord, "Behold, I will make them of the synagogue of Satan, which say *they are Jews*, and are not, but do lie; behold, I will make them to come and worship before thy feet, and to know that I have loved thee."

Sec. 6.—Jacob. (*Chap. xxvi.* 34–*xxxvii.* 1.)

The Dispensational Application.—In Isaac we have had, as we have seen already, the acknowledged type of the Son of God. In the twenty-second chapter also Abraham takes the place, which from his relationship we are prepared to find him filling, the place of the typical father. These two, Abraham and Isaac, God links with Jacob's name when revealing Himself to Moses at the bush He bids him "say unto the children of Israel, 'The God of Abraham, and the God of Isaac, and the God of Jacob hath sent me to you.'" This is, as the apostle tells us, a sign of His approbation of them: "God was not ashamed to be called their God;" He could connect His name openly with theirs. Had He said He was the God of Lot, Lot's conduct would have been His own dishonor. The special choice of these three men in the way God chose to associate them with Himself was perhaps the highest honor He could bestow upon men.

In the New Testament there is one name which has of necessity displaced all other names. God has found one Man with whom He can perfectly and forever identify Himself, and from whom His character can be fully learned. He has been revealed in His Son, and is now to us forever known as the "God and Father of our Lord Jesus Christ."

But surely this will prepare us to see even in the case of the Old-Testament names a deeper view of God than any thing which could be gathered merely from their biographies. As to two of them, we have seen that this is justified by the fact; but God, when linking in His revelation to Moses the

name of Jacob with this, adds, "This is My name
forever, and this is My memorial unto all generations." This has generally been limited to the title,
"Jehovah," which is the word our version, as is
well known, here as almost always, translates as
"Lord," but which is, indeed, almost identical with
the "I am" of the previous verse: "I am hath sent
me to you." Nor can it be for a moment contested
that Jehovah is the name by which God is henceforth known as Israel's covenant-God. This is not
meant, then, to be disputed. Only along with and
displaying this "Eternal" One, this other term
comes in: "Jehovah, God of your fathers, the God
of Abraham, and the God of Isaac, and the God
of Jacob: this"—all of it—"is My name forever,
and this is My memorial unto all generations."

For us the God of redemption is indeed here
fully displayed. For if in Abraham we find manifestly the type of the Father, and in Isaac admit-
tedly that of the Son, in Jacob-Israel we find a
type and pattern of the Spirit's work which is
again and again dwelt on and expanded in the
after-scriptures. Balaam's words as to the people,
using this double—this natural and this spiritual—
name, are surely as true of the nation's ancestors,
"It shall be said of Jacob and of Israel, What
hath God wrought!" What God hath wrought is
surely what in the one now before us we are called
in an especial way to acknowledge and glory in.
For Jacob's God is He whom we still know as ac-
complishing in us by almighty power the purposes
of sovereign grace.   •

In these two names of his—Jacob and Israel—
the key to all his history is found. The long years
of discipline through which he passes are necessi-

tated by his being Jacob: they are the necessary
result of righteous government, but which in the
hands of a God infinitely gracious issue in blessing
the most signal to the chastened soul; the worm
Jacob becomes, in the consciousness of his weakness, Israel,—has power with God and with man
and prevails. The fruitfulness of God's holy discipline is surely the moral of his life.

And of this the nation are as striking an example. The only people chosen of God as His own
among the nations of the earth to be the manifest
seat of divine government, their own history becomes of necessity the illustration of this. "You
only have I known," He says, "of all the families
of the earth; *therefore* I will punish you for your
iniquities." Any thing else but this would have
been impossible for a holy God. And yet it is of
Israel and their election that it is said, "The gifts
and calling of God are without repentance." (Rom.
xi. 29.) Even in their present state of dispersion,
as the apostle argues, they are still "beloved for
the fathers' sakes." Their rejection as a nation is
not final. God repudiates utterly, by the mouth
of Jeremiah, that which is still the thought of
many Christians: "Considerest thou not what this
people have spoken, saying, 'The two families
which the Lord hath chosen, He hath even cut
them off'? Thus have they despised My people,
that they should be no more a nation before them.
Thus saith the Lord, If My covenant be not with
day and night, and if I have not appointed the
ordinances of heaven and earth, then will I cast
away the seed of Jacob, and David My servant, so
that I will not take any of his seed to be rulers
over the seed of Abraham, Isaac, and Jacob; for

I will cause their captivity to return, and have
mercy on them." (Jer. xxxiii. 24–26.)

Their present chastening is therefore for final
reformation, and thus nationally are they a pattern
of God's dealings in holiness, but in grace, with all
His people. Their father Jacob becomes thus also
their type, a view to which it seems to me the language of the prophets every where conforms, and
which it indeed necessitates.

The life of Jacob divides into three parts, according as we find him in the land, exiled from it
at Padan-Aram, or again returning; and to this
correspond very plainly the three great periods of
Israel's national life. The last is indeed only
known by prophecy, but as surely as any history
could make it known.

The first part seems to me to cover the whole
of their inspired history. Jacob is shown to us, as
the apostle declares in Romans ix, as the object of
election. The constant order of Genesis is, as we
have seen, the rejection of the first-born: it is
"first that which is natural, and afterward that
which is spiritual." But in every other case there
is some plain reason for the divine choice. In
Cain, self-righteousness sets aside; in Isaac, his
birth from Sarah might be urged as reason; Reu-
ben, too, falls into sin, which deprives him of the
birthright. In Jacob's case, as the apostle tells us,
"The children being not yet born, neither having
done any good or evil, that the purpose of God
according to election might stand, not of works,
but of Him that calleth; it was said unto her, 'The
elder shall serve the younger.'" Jacob stands
indeed here scarcely so much as a type of the
people as he is one with the people: "Jacob have

I loved " is said of both. And this choice of divine love, as it insures their full final blessing, so it insures the discipline needed as the demand of His holiness and of that blessing of theirs also: "You only have I known of all the families of the earth; therefore I will punish you for your iniquities."   Beth-el, the house of God, figures therefore so largely in Jacob's history, and it is as El Beth-el, the God of His own house, that he has to know Him, in the holiness which becomes His house.   It is thus at Beth-el, when he returns there, that his history morally closes.

In this first part he answers fully to the name which Esau indignantly invokes: "Is he not rightly called Jacob? for he hath supplanted me these two times."   The national characteristic cannot be well doubted here.   Jacob values the blessing of God, but seeks it in subtle and carnal ways, totally opposed to faith, as the apostle testifies of Israel that they "sought after the law of righteousness," but "did not attain to the law of righteousness; and wherefore? Because they sought it not by faith."   It was thus they stumbled at the stumbling-stone, and became wanderers from the land of promise, exiled by their sin.   Yet as Jacob, an exile from his father's house, finds God at Beth-el watching over him with providential care, and assuring him of a final return to his father's house in peace, so have his seed been watched over in all their wanderings, and their return to their land is guaranteed by the sure word of prophecy.

The Lord in His words to Nathanael applies that Beth-el vision to Himself.   It is when Israel shall accept with Nathanael's faith the Lord Jesus Christ as Son of God and King of Israel that they shall have the blessedness of looking up into an opened heavens, and seeing the angels of God, in their ministrations to men, attending on the Son of Man; and these two thoughts combined—Son of God, as confessed by Nathanael, and Son of Man, as in His love to men He constantly styled Himself—imply a Beth-el, a house of God on earth. In that day it could be but a vision of the future, for the nation had not Nathanael's faith. For such as he, the pledge of that day was already there.

During Jacob's twenty years at Padan-Aram he enjoys no further revelation until the angel of God bids him depart thence. In the meantime He deals with him as one for whom He has purposes of blessing which can be reached only through disciplinary toil and sorrow. He is multiplied through unwelcome Leah and the two bondmaids mainly, serving long and with hard labor for his wives and flocks. The general application to such a history as that of Israel since her dispersion is not difficult to make, although it may be impossible to trace in detail. Perhaps we should expect no more than a general thought of such a history, as the Spirit of God could find nothing in it upon which to dwell, save only to magnify the divine mercy in it. Enslaved, trampled on, yet preserved, and merging into final wealth and power: this is the simple, well-known, yet marvelous fact, in which they witness to the care and holiness of that God of Beth-el whose name they know not.

In the third part we find Jacob (up to this, still and only that,) returning to his own land. In the application, we must remember that it is a remnant that represent and grow into the nation. For these as for their father, Peniel prepares for Beth-el; that they may not fall into their enemies' hands, God, whose name is yet unknown to them, must take them into His own, crippling the human strength in which they contend with Him, that in weakness they may hold Him fast for blessing. They must needs confess their name naturally, that grace may change it for what has to be hence-forth their name. At Peniel, Jacob becomes Israel, although not yet does he fully realize that which is implied in this, so that at Beth-el he again receives it, as if never his before. Thus, broken down in repentance, and their human strength abased, the nation will be saved from the hands of their enemies. Purged from idolatry, they will then have their second Beth-el, when God dis-covers to them His name, so long hidden, and confirms to them the promise to their father Abraham. Christ, Son of His mother's sorrow, but of His Father's right hand, will then take His place among them, and so they will come to Mamre, and to Hebron, to the richness of a por-tion which now is to be enjoyed in fellowship with God.

The Individual Application.—In the individual application the lesson of Jacob's life is, as we have already seen, the fruitfulness of that holy discipline which Beth-el, the house of God, implies, and which out of such material as a Jacob can bring forth a vessel of exquisite workmanship to His praise. Here the literal history unites with the typical to develop a picture of the deepest interest to us. May He who only can, give us true blessing from it.

First, as a preface to the setting aside of Esau, we are told of his marriage, at forty years old, at once to two Canaanitish wives. This is the natural sequel of a profanity which could esteem his birthright at the value of a mess of pottage. These "forty years" are a significant hint to us of completed probation. In his two wives, married at once, he refuses at once the example and counsel of his father, and by his union with Canaanitish women disregards the divine sentence, and shows unmistakably the innermost recesses of the heart. It is a sign of the times that so little is thought of the character of man's associations. In truth, nothing gives us our character so much. To say of Enoch, or of Noah, that "he walked with God," describes the man fully in the fewest words; voluntary association with His enemies, can it consist with any proper desire after such a walk? Esau's Canaanitish wives set him finally aside from the blessing which the next chapter shows us becoming Jacob's.

On the other hand, crookedness and deceit are found in Jacob, the vices which belong to feebleness where there is no due counteracting power of faith. Faith, which alone is wisdom and foresight,

waits upon God and makes no haste. It walks
erect and openly in the shelter of His presence
secure of the accomplishment of His will, which
alone it seeks, while cunning and craft blunder in
the darkness. Jacob's deceit is not that which procures him the blessing: it procures him nothing
but twenty years of toil and sorrow, of banishment
from his father's house, and subjection to the will
of others. The blessing could not be Esau's. Was
Isaac or Esau more than God that they could alter
His purpose? or did He need Jacob's feeble hand
to uphold His throne? Alas! he is neither the
first nor the last who has acted as if it were so.
And this is what restlessness and impatience mean,
—either some lust of the heart we must secure
whether He will or no, or some doubt whether
God be God:—rank unbelief or rank self-will;
and these are near companions. How far off was
Jacob yet from El-Beth-el!

True, there was strong temptation,—a mother's
voice, the voice of affection and authority, to urge
him on; the coveted blessing just slipping, as it
seemed, away: but in the case of one with God,
all this would only have made plain the power of
God to keep a soul that confides in Him. With
Him, no difficulties avail against us; it is not inherent strength or wisdom which avails in our
behalf. The whole question is, Are we with Him?

Jacob feebly opposes his mother's solicitation,
but not in the name of God or of truth. He dreads
getting a curse instead of blessing,—"*seeming* a
deceiver," rather than being one. He makes the
whole question one of expediency, not of righteousness, hence has no power at all, or rather is
already fallen. His mother boldly assumes the

responsibility, and he has nothing more to oppose.

Once gained, he soon learns boldness; he can not only assure his father, once and again, that he is Esau, but dares to say that God has brought him what Rebekah's hands have prepared. What is holiness in us but the fruit of the shining of God's face upon us? If our faces are turned away, how soon does all the rabble of evil stalk abroad in the darkness! "The fruit of the *light* is in all goodness and righteousness and truth." (Eph. v. 9, true reading.)

Yet Jacob obtains the blessing, surely from grace alone, and not from his evil works; and Isaac, dim-sighted spiritually more than physically here, wakes up to find how far nature has misled him, and to own the righteousness of a stronger will than his own. Esau sees nothing but Jacob and his father.

He who has now got the blessing is still totally without ability to trust God for the fulfillment of it. Rebekah's voice again is heard, urging him to flee from his brother's wrath, and Isaac is wrought upon to send him to Padan-Aram, to take a wife from Laban's daughters. It is now that solitary, a wanderer and a fugitive, he arrives at Beth-el, and here for the first time God appears to him.

Already the chastening of God's hand was upon him, and heavily he must have felt it as he lay upon the hill that night at Luz. Under the pressure of it, he was now to have the interpretation as the holy discipline of divine love. He must stoop his neck to the yoke, and accept the fruit of his own ways; God can assure him of no escape from that: but in and through it all the blessing that is his shall be attained. He will be with him to accomplish His faithful word, and bring him back from all his wanderings into the land which he is now leaving. He sees the angels of God passing between heaven and earth in constant ministration to the heir of promise, for He whom they serve is Abraham's God.

Here all is perfect grace, for grace alone de-livers from the dominion of sin. Holiness is the necessary rule of God's house, but to be in God's house supposes relationship,—nearness. Jacob's matters, wonderful to say, are God's own care. What a remedy for Jacob's self-seeking anxiety is in all this! Had he learnt the lesson, how much evil would have been spared him! how soon and how differently might Peniel have been reached! But it is evident he enters little into the spirit of this divine communication. He calls the place in-deed Beth-el, God's house, and the gate of heaven, but he is oppressed with fear, rather than com-forted. The magnificence of the promise which has just been made him shrinks into mere bread and raiment, and his father's house again in peace, and he answers with a legal vow, in which what *he* will do is all too manifest. So he goes on his journey to find in Laban's house what is more congenial yet than God's, and to learn slowly there by experience what faith might have learnt as speedily as surely, without the sorrow.

In all this Jacob is our type; for if he were re-sponsible to receive and walk in the power of a grace so plainly revealed, how much more we who have received a revelation which is to Jacob's as noon to twilight! To us the God of Abraham and of Isaac is the God and Father of our Lord Jesus Christ, and through Him our Father. For

us the house of God is found on earth, all the fullness of God dwelling bodily in the Man Christ
Jesus; and the promise, "I will dwell in them and
walk in them," being fulfilled to us also, as indi-
vidually and collectively indwelt by the Holy
Ghost. For us the throne of God is revealed as
a throne of grace,—grace reigning through righteousness; our Saviour, Christ our Lord. How
should all this purge out of our souls the leaven
of subtilty and self-will, and conform us wholly to
the will of God! "His commandments are not
grievous," says the apostle: what say our souls?
Practically, as day by day His will is declared, is
it the conviction of our hearts, and what our lives
manifest, that His yoke is easy and His burden
light?

In fact it is more: it is the only true and practical rest for the soul, and the test of how far our
hearts have been brought back to God. "Faith, if
it have not works, is dead, being alone." "Whoso
keepeth His word, in him verily is the love of God
perfected; hereby know we that we are in Him."
It is divine love which, sown in the heart, produces
in the life the necessary fruit of service. Faith is
the heart's response; service, the life's. Nor can the
one be very much below the measure of the other.

Grace is that which, in the knowledge of it, de-
livers from our own will and ways. We cannot,
blessed be God, carry it too far or rejoice in it too
fully. He whose life is unfruitful testifies (whatever his lips affirm) how little he has known of it,
not that he has carried it too far, or abandoned
himself to it too entirely. That is impossible. "Sin
shall *not* have dominion over you, *because* ye are
not under the law, but under grace."

"Then Jacob went on his journey, and came into the land of the children of the east." And here the second period of his life begins. He is now a stranger, a servant for hire, the victim of deceit and self-aggrandizement on the part of Laban, his relative, and morally also near akin. It is impossible to mistake the retribution all the way through, in which the measure he has meted to another is measured to himself again; but it is impossible also not to see that in the manner in which it is dealt out God is speaking to the heart and conscience of the wanderer. There is governmental equity, but also the chastening of a holy love. Beth-el is vindicating itself. The Father scourgeth every son whom He receiveth. The sceptre of the kingdom is the rod of discipline of the Father's house.

Deceit and injustice practiced upon ourselves, how easy to read them in their true character! how the poor pretense of justification we had attempted in our own behalf betrays its shame when another attempts it against us. Thus can God overrule sin to teach us holiness. Yet the lesson this way is long in learning, as we surely see in Jacob. Throughout it he is Jacob still, though by degrees becoming fruitful and prosperous.

The general teaching here seems plain enough, while the details are difficult to follow. The names of wives and children too bear witness to the subjective character of the line of truth which presents itself to us. Rachel, "sheep," seems significant of the meekness and patience of true discipleship, the very opposite of Jacob's hitherto self-willed and unrestrained temper. But her he must obtain by means of undesired Leah, whose name, "wearied," suggests the "tribulation" by which "patience" is wrought out. And even then, before Rachel is fruitful, and in despair of her fruitfulness, the bondmaids are received, Bilhah, "terror," and Zilpah, a "dropping" (as of tears).

These names seem to harmonize very strikingly with the general purport of the history. Indeed, putting them together, they carry conviction scarcely to be resisted. The names of the children, again, as they should do, speak on the other hand of various blessing, but which I am not prepared to enter into here. But Joseph, Rachel's son, surely, in beautiful conformity to his origin, expresses that steady "virtue" (or courage) which goes through whatever trial to the crown, and with which Peter commences that spiritual "adding" to which he exhorts (2 Pet. i. 5), and which seems indicated in Joseph's name. From *his* birth Jacob begins to look toward his own place and country once more; and though at Laban's request he continues six years longer in his service, he yet now emerges from the poverty in which he has for so long been, until his riches awaken the envy of Laban's sons and of their father. Yet he waits until Jehovah's voice bids him return to the land of his fathers, though still lacking faith to take an open course—he steals secretly away, God interposing to save him from the pursuit of Laban, who follows him to Gilead, but there to part from him with a solemn covenant.

Jacob now pursues his way, and angels of God meet him: how ready is He to assure us of His power waiting only a fit moment to be put forth in our behalf! It must have reminded, and been intended to remind him too, of Beth-el, and of the

promise there; but there Jehovah had appeared to
him, if but in a dream. Here He does not appear.
Jacob an outcast and wanderer could have that
which Jacob returning in wealth aud with a multitude could not now be permitted. Then, it was
grace; now, it would be fellowship; and for fellowship he was not yet prepared. "This is God's
host," (or "camp,") he says; and he calls the place
"Mahanaim,"—that is, "*two* hosts," or "camps."
Here he must have counted in his own, and ac-
cordingly we find him immediately dwelling upon
it in his message to Esau: "I have oxen and asses,
flocks and men-servants and women-servants, and
I have sent to tell my lord, that I may find favor
in thy sight." How significant that in but a little
time we find him dividing this host of his into *two
camps*,* saying, "If Esau come to the one camp*
and smite it, then the other camp* which is left
shall escape"! Such is our strength when built
upon, although we would fain perhaps associate
God's power with it. In the time of need, our
own, what is it? and God's, where shall we
find it?

It is remarkable too that it is just when he has
met God's messengers† that he sends his own to
Seir to Esau. But God and Esau are evidently
mixed up in his mind all through. Nor is it
strange, but inevitable, that what recalls God to
our souls should recall also one against whom we
have sinned, and sinned without reparation; perhaps without possibility of reparation. Beth-el is
still manifesting itself in all this—the discipline
which becomes God's holy house. There was but
too much truth hid under Jacob's servile words to

---

* The same word as before.   † Same word as "angels."

his brother a little later: "I have seen thy face as though I had seen the face of God."

Yet when he said this, Peniel had intervened; and he had "called the name of the place Peniel, because [he said,] I have seen God face to face." How could he *after that* fail to distinguish between God's face and his brother's.

He could not, had Peniel really answered to its name; but how often do we misinterpret the significance of what has been (as Peniel was to Jacob) of most real importance to our souls! Had he seen God in reality "face to face," how could he have added to this as the wonderful thing (as we find him doing,) "and *my life is preserved*"? Who that *has* seen God's face but has found in it deliverance from self-occupation and from fear, such as controlled Jacob when he met his brother?

God had indeed met Jacob, but met him by night and not by day: when the day broke He had disappeared. And correspondingly, though He blessed him finally, He refused to declare His name to Jacob's entreaty. Unknown He had come and unknown He departed.

Jacob it was who had acquired a name at Peniel, and yet even this cannot be said without reserve; for at Beth-el afterward he has afresh to receive it, —there where Beth-el itself for the first time really acquires its name. These two things are surely connected. What he has learned at Peniel is expressed in his altar at Shechem, where he proclaims exultingly God to be the God of Israel—*his* God; but his altar at Beth-el owns Him God of His own house, in which in subjection Israel must find his place in order to have really the power of his name.

At Peniel God meets him (His face hidden) to
make him learn the strength which is perfected
only in weakness. With his thigh out of joint he
prevails and is blessed. The secret of strength is
learned, and yet, strange as it may seem, the power
that he has with God he cannot yet find before
man. He meets Esau with abject servility, prac-
tices still his old deceit, talks of following him to
Seir, and as soon as freed from his presence,
crosses into Canaan, building him a house at Suc-
coth, and buying a parcel of ground at Shechem.
There he proclaims God as God of Israel, when
presently Dinah falls, and the massacre of the
Shechemites makes him quake with fear because
of the inhabitants of the land. No part of his
history is so dark and shameful as that which
follows the scene in which (and they are divine
words) "as a prince he has power with God *and
with men*, and prevails."

If this be a mystery, it is one with which the experience of the saint is but too familiar. Power
may be ours which yet we cannot manifest, or find
for our emergencies. "I besought Thy disciples to
cast him out, and they could not," says the father
of the possessed. And those to whom this very
power had been committed ask in perplexity,
"Why could not we cast him out?" And the
Lord replies, "Because of your unbelief;" but
adds, "Howbeit this kind goeth not forth but by
prayer and fasting."

Even so he whose name is already Israel is practically Jacob still, as God says to him afterward
(xxxv. 10). Only in obedience can power be used;
our meat and drink—our strength and refreshment
—are in doing His will; grace, where realized,

breaks the dominion of sin; and "sin is lawless-ness," our own will and not His. Divine power *must* be realized in the divine *ways:* grace only establishes, never alters this. So at Beth-el alone the promise of Peniel can be fulfilled.

How many are there whose altars are to "God their God," and who exult in a grace which proves yet no practical deliverance; who dwell in an unpurged earth, and are reaping, and must be allowed to reap, the sure and bitter fruits! God's princes, how far from knowing the dignity of their calling!

In the extremity of his distress God's voice arouses Jacob to "go up to Beth-el and dwell there;" and then we hear of strange gods in his household to be put away, and purification effected to meet Him "who answered me in the day of my distress, and was with me in the way I went;" and the terror of God falls upon the cities round about, so that they do not pursue after the sons of Jacob. At Beth-el his wanderings really end; his new name is confirmed to him, and God declares His own, as at Peniel He could not; the blessing now is fully his; and Jacob bowed in gratitude recognizes the house of God, in which (the pur-pose of discipline being accomplished,) he finds at last his rest.

Still he journeys on, for pilgrimage is not over, although in the land now, his portion. Sorrow still comes, for on the road to Bethlehem his be-loved Rachel dies, but Jacob now shows his mastery over it. Him whom his dying mother names Ben-oni, "son of my affliction," his father calls Benjamin, "son of the right hand." We can easily discern the reflection of Christ in this, the glory fruit of the cross. With our eye on this, Mamre, which is in Hebron, (the "richness of communion,") Abraham's old resting-place, is soon reached. With how great toil and how many experiences is he back at last, whence only unbelief had ever driven him! And we? how much do most of us resemble him in this! Yet with him and us "tribulation worketh patience, and patience experience, and experience hope, and hope maketh not ashamed."

The next chapter follows with a long list of Esau's generations, prematurely ripening into dukes and kings. The world must have its day; and yet amid it all a significant sign is given of fulfillment of that divine purpose "which is not of works, but of Him that calleth;" for we read that "Esau took his wives, and his sons, and his daughters, and all the persons of his house, and his cattle and his beasts, and all his substance, which he had got in the land of Canaan, and *went into the country from the face of his brother Jacob*."

While in chapter xxxvii. one verse contrasts Jacob's portion, its very brevity speaking volumes to the ear that hears:—

"And Jacob dwelt in the land in which his father was a stranger, in the land of Canaan."

Sec. 7.—Joseph. (Chap. xxxvii. 2–l.)

The Dispensational Application.—Joseph, whose touching history closes the book before us, is so well known as a type of the Lord that there is no need to insist upon the reality of the application. It is one of the longest, fullest, and clearest to be found in Scripture; and here, as we have seen before in another case, the inward, individual application seems almost to be absorbed by and make way for the outward. Nor need we wonder: for in these stages of the divine life in man we have now reached that in which finally the fruit of the new nature, its proper and characteristic fruit, is found, and here it is no longer I that live, but "Christ liveth in me."

The first view that we have of Joseph is at seventeen years feeding the flock along with his brethren. How ever the typical ruler for God is the shepherd! of Moses and of David both we find this; and in Matthew (the kingdom-gospel) we hear the scribes quoting Micah to the king: "Out of thee shall come a Governor who shall rule My people Israel." In the margin this is "feed;" it is literally "be a shepherd to" My people Israel. Jacob's prophecy at the close of this book connects this character of Christ's rule with the type of Joseph (xlix. 24).

It is with the children of the bondmaid too that we find him,—a significant expression of Israel's condition, politically perhaps as well as spiritually, when the Lord came in flesh; but separated from them morally far, the ground of the after-separation upon their side, not on His. "Me the world

hateth," said the Lord to His brethren, "because
I testify of it that its deeds are evil."

Special object of his father's love, and prophet
of his own coming exaltation, he incurs through
all this an intensity of enmity which finds its op
portunity in his mission of love as sent of his father
to them.   He seeks them in Shechem, finds them
in Dothan, and there in brethren after the flesh, in
will and intent, murderers.   But these names, like
all others in Scripture, are suggestive; and it is
surely in place to inquire what they suggest.

Now Shechem we have already had twice before
us, and it seems referred to again in chap. xlviii. 22.
It is here translated "portion;" a meaning which
in Scripture it never elsewhere has: its undoubted
uniform sense is "shoulder," which is usually considered to refer to the "position of the place on
the 'saddle' or 'shoulder' of the heights which
divide the waters there that flow to the Mediterranean on the west and to the Jordan on the east." *
There is no need to exclude this significance, any
more than to stop here as if it were the whole
matter.   The natural constantly typifies the spiritual; and so it may well be in this case.

Figuratively the shoulder finds its place as the
burden-bearer, and this with the thought of service
and subjection as in the blessing of Issachar afterward: "He bowed his shoulder to bear, and became a servant unto tribute;" but the burden may
be one of a very different character, as it is said of
the Lord, "The government shall be upon His
shoulder:" the place of service and the place of
power being here one.   How truly so of Him
whom this declares!

_____

*Smith's Dictionary of the Bible.

In the first case in which we have to do with Shechem, I have sought to show that we have the former thought. The oak of Moreh (the "instructor") at the ·"place of Sichem," Abraham's first resting-place in the land, gives beautifully the fruitfulness of subjection to divine teaching; and here Jehovah Himself appears to him. We need seek no further for the significance of Shechem in the history of Joseph's brethren. From Abraham's place Abraham's seed had but too far wandered when the Lord came as seeking them. Zealous law-keepers they were, and to this Dothan, if I mistake not, very exactly points. It means "laws," in the sense, not of "precepts," (moral—spiritual—guidance, such as the divine law was,) but of imperial "decrees."* To Israel, away from God and from the path of their father after the flesh, such had the divine word become.

At Dothan, then, Joseph's brethren are found, and at once they counsel to slay him. In fact they cast him into a pit, but which holds no water—"It is not lawful for us," the Jews said to Pilate, "to put any man to death;"—and out of this they draw him to sell him to the Ishmaelites for twenty pieces of silver. So by Israel was the Lord transferred to the Gentiles.

How striking is that touch in this terrible picture, "And they sat down"—with Joseph in their pit—"to eat bread"! How much more terrible in the case of the pharisaic persecutors who "would not go into the judgment-hall, lest they should be defiled, but that they might eat the passover"! History does indeed repeat itself, because each

---

*"Dothan" is generally held to mean "two cisterns" or "wells;" some, however, prefer the meaning "laws," from *dath*, a very different word from *torah*, (akin to Moreh above,) the usual word for Jehovah's "law."

generation but repeats the one before it: as Ahab, Israel's worst king, was but after all what his name signifies, his "father's brother."

Thus Joseph is brought down into Egypt; but before his history is proceeded with, that of Judah, terrible record as it is, is continued through another chapter (xxxviii). That it is simply *Judah's* history is itself significant. Israel (the ten tribes) have for long had none; the Jews for us represent the whole people. Here at the outset Judah separates himself from his brethren and connects himself with the Canaanite,—the "merchantman,"—marrying the daughter of Shuah (or "riches"). Surely these names give us in plain speech the characteristics of the nation for these centuries since the cross! His seed is thus, however, continued upon the earth, although God's wrath is upon the first two sons, (whose names speak, Er, of "enmity," and Onan, of "iniquity,") while the *third* son, Shelah, ("sprout"?) speaks of divine power in resurrection bringing out of death.* Thus is a remnant preserved.

The history of Tamar shows us in God's own marvelous way how Christ comes into connection with Judah, and thus it is her name appears in the Lord's genealogy in the gospel of Matthew, first of those four women's names, whose presence there demonstrates the grace which has stooped to take up men. Each of these four has its own distinctive gospel-feature to bring out, as has been elsewhere shown.† It is Tamar's *sin* that is insisted on, as it

---

*"Come, and let us return unto the Lord: for He hath torn, and He will heal us; He hath smitten, and He will bind us up. After two days He will revive us: in the third day He will raise us up, and we shall live in His sight." (Hos. vi. 1, 2.)

†"The Women of the Genealogy," first published in "*The Present Testimony.*"

is Rahab's *faith;* while for Ruth to come in, the
sentence of the law has to be set aside, and Bath-
sheba shows us grace triumphing even over a
believer's sin. A salvation for sinners,—a salvation by faith,—a salvation from the sentence
of the law,—an *eternal* salvation: this is what the
simple insertion of these names declares. And
in this chapter of Genesis, whatever else may
be contained, we are assured, as every where,
for Jew first, and for Gentile also, *sin* it is
which through the infinite pity of God connects
us with a *Saviour.* Tamar's sin alone brought
her into the Lord's genealogy; and God has
taken pains to record, doubly record, this striking fact. Even so as simply sinners have we
title to rejoice in a work accomplished for the
need of sinners. Judah shall find in a coming
day his title, not in legal righteousness, nor in
Abrahamic descent, but in what God has emphasized for us here.

With chap. xxxix. we come back to Joseph,—in
type, to see Christ among the Gentiles. It is evident that thus viewed there is no direct continuity
with the thirty-seventh chapter, but in some sort a
new beginning. Even the position of Joseph under
an Egyptian master may remind us of Zechariah's
words, which I believe with others to be intended
of Christ: "Man acquired me as a slave from my
youth" (ch. xiii. 5, *Heb.*). Here, notice, it is not
Israel: the lowly service to which He has stooped
has the widest scope. Of course He is at the same
time, and always, Jehovah's perfect servant: the
one thing, far from being inconsistent with the
other, involved it. But what response did this
service receive from man? " What are those

wounds in Thine hands? Those with which I was wounded in the house of My friends."

With Joseph in it, the house of the Egyptian is blessed of God; but with Christ ministering in it, how unspeakably was the world blessed! All the power was there, and manifesting itself, which could have turned, and will yet turn, the need of man, however great and varied, into occasion for the display of the wealth of divine loving-mercy. But it availed not to turn man's heart to God: false witness casts Joseph into Pharaoh's prison, where, however, all things come into his hand; while under false accusation the Lord descends into a darker prison-house, in result to manifest Himself as Master of all there.

A higher power than man's was working beneath all this in Joseph's case. The path of humiliation was to end for him in glory; the sorrow of the way was to issue in the joy—love's own joy of service in a higher sphere. "God did send me before you to preserve life," he says to his brethren afterward; and he who in prison reveals himself as the interpreter of the mind of God, is as such qualified to administer the resources of the throne of Egypt for the relief of the distress which is at hand for the world. All this is easily read as typical of the Lord, only that the shadows of the picture are immeasurably darker here, as the lights are inexpressibly brighter. From the humiliation and agony of the cross, in which He is the interpreter of man's just doom on the one hand and of the mercy for him on the other, the lowly Minister to human need comes forth to serve as Wisdom and Power of God upon a throne of grace. She-chem is the portion of **our Joseph's inheritance,** for a better kingdom than any kingdom of the nations is that He receives. (Mark x. 42.)

Seven years of plenty to be succeeded by seven years of famine which shall devour them up,—such is the prophecy of Pharaoh's dream. Even yet is the world enjoying its plenteous years, and little it believes in its plainly predicted future. The time of famine is nevertheless surely not far off which is to manifest the resources of Him who will then be seen alone competent to meet its terrible exigencies. In that sore time of trial both Israel are to be brought back to Him whom they have rejected, and the world to be subjected to the throne whose provision of grace He ministers. These things are now in our type with some detail set before us.

But first, and as soon as ever he is exalted, we hear of new relationships for Joseph: "And Pharaoh called Joseph's name Zaphnath-paaneah; and he gave him to wife Asenath the daughter of Poti-pherah priest of On; and Joseph went out over all the land of Egypt." The name given we may take as Hebrew,* and in the meaning anciently given to it, "Revealer of Secrets." How precious a title for Him who has indeed revealed to us the secrets of the heart of God! And especially is it appropriate typically in connection (as the text suggests) with Joseph's Gentile marriage. To Christianity belongs, above all, the revelation of the divine "mysteries." The "mysteries of the

---

* The absurdity does not follow which Grove suggests (*Smith's Dict. of the Bible*) that it makes Pharaoh speak in Hebrew. If it has pleased God to speak to us in Hebrew, why should not the Egyptian name be translated into this to make it intelligible to us? I am not convinced of the wisdom of seeking the meaning of these names in ancient and little-known tongues, and these "Shemiticized;" at least when the Hebrew furnishes a satisfactory one nearer at hand.

kingdom," the "great mystery" of "Christ and the Church;" the "mystery of His will . . . for the administration of the fullness of times, to head up all things in the heavens and earth in Christ" (Matt. xiii. 11; Eph. v. 32, i. 9, 10) are given to us for the first time in these Christian days; while He Himself is, in His own person and work, the "mystery of godliness." Even the false church appropriates (only to pervert) this idea of "mystery" (Rev. xvii. 5); while the apostle desires no better estimation for himself and others than "as ministers of Christ, and stewards of the mysteries of God" (1 Cor. iv. 1). For us, even the stored treasures of the past dispensation are revealing themselves, and things which happened unto Israel happened unto them for types, and are written for our admonition upon whom the ends of the ages are come (1 Cor. x. 11). All these things are pledges of new relationship, confidences (how unspeakably precious!) of the heart of Christ (Jno. xv. 15). Revealer of secrets indeed is He; no truer or sweeter name for Him who has been pleased to take, in these plenteous days before the time of the world's famine, a Gentile bride.

As to Asenath, if the meaning of her name is conjectural only,* yet those of her two sons are very significant. Born before the famine, and while Joseph's brethren are yet strangers to his exaltation, he "called the name of the first-born Manasseh: For God hath made me forget all my toil, and all my father's house;" while "the name of the second called he Ephraim: For God hath

---

*According to Poole (*Smith's Dict.*), probably "storehouse;" but Simonis, with the help of the Ethiopic, suggests "beauty." The old conjecture, "worshiper of Neith," every way objectionable, is generally given up.

made me fruitful in the land of my affliction."
Here, clearly, is our place and relationship with
our blessed Lord; and how blessed to realize the
value to Him of which these names speak. For
His Church, His heavenly bride, He has been
content to be as if He remembered not His relationship with His people of old. The thread of
prophecy lies unwoven on the shuttle of time, as if
its wheel had stopped forever. What means this
attitude of forgetfulness on the part of Him who
neither slumbereth nor sleepeth? Surely no
change, but the pursuance of eternal purposes,
which accomplished, Israel shall look upon the
face of Him whom they have pierced, and a
fountain be opened to them also for sin and for
uncleanness.

So "the seven years of plenteousness, that was
in the land of Egypt, were ended. And the seven
years of dearth began to come, ... and the
dearth was in all lands. . . . . And when all the
land of Egypt was famished, the people cried to
Pharaoh for bread: and Pharaoh said unto all the
Egyptians, 'Go unto Joseph; what he saith to
you, do.'"

So when God's judgments are in the earth, the
inhabitants of the world will learn righteousness.
It is face to face with our need that we learn our
true nothingness, and cry out to Him who then
proves Himself the living God. But God's remedy is Christ alone. He has put, absolutely and
unrepentingly, all things in His hand. He would
have all men to be saved, but there is no other
name given whereby we can be saved. As for the
individual, so for the world: not in the plenteous
times of Christianity will the world at large turn

to God; and therefore come drought and famine from the same hand that, unknown, bestowed the blessing.

The present dispensation closed by the removal of the Church to be with her Head and Lord, the times of the Gentiles will close as the Lord Himself predicts: "And there shall be signs in the sun and in the moon and in the stars; and upon the earth distress of nations with perplexity, the sea and the waves roaring; men's hearts failing them for fear, and for looking after those things which are coming on the earth; for the powers of heaven shall be shaken. And then shall they see the Son of Man coming in a cloud with power and great glory." (Luke xxi. 25–27.)

But before He appears, and amid all the trial of a time such as the world has never seen—will never again see,—Israel will be preparing to recognize and receive her rejected Lord. "Ask ye now, and see whether a man doth travail with child? wherefore do I see every man with his hands on his loins, as a woman in travail, and all faces are turned into paleness? Alas! for that day is great, so that none is like it; it is even the time of Jacob's trouble; but he shall be saved out of it, and . . . . they shall serve the Lord their God, and David their king, whom I will raise up unto them" (Jer. xxx. 6, 7, 9). It is indeed the travail-time of Israel's new birth.

In the type before us, the famine reaches Canaan, as all the countries around, and Joseph's ten brethren come down to buy corn in Egypt. We are all familiar with what follows, and how their hearts and consciences are probed by him who knows them and loves them well, but whom they know not. They obtain indeed a temporary supply for their necessities, but leave Simeon in prison, and are bidden not to appear again except they bring Benjamin with them. Famine again forces them to come down, and this time, Judah having undertaken for Benjamin with his father, they bring him also; are then feasted by Joseph still unknown; sent away with the cup in Benjamin's sack; pursued and brought back under the charge of theft; Benjamin is to remain as Joseph's slave, but Judah, his heart fully reached, offers himself in his stead: then Joseph's love bursts out; he makes himself known to them; they own their sin, are reconciled and comforted with his love.

In all this it is plain how every thing turns on Benjamin and their state toward him. This is made the test of their condition. The power for their deliverance lies in Joseph's hands alone, however, and their exercises as to Benjamin all tend to awakening conscience and heart as to their sin against Joseph. The key of the typical interpretation is to be found in this.*

Joseph is, as we know, Christ once rejected and suffering, now exalted: this is He whom Israel does not know. A Christ triumphant simply and reigning upon earth is the Benjamin who is found among them, whether in the days of the Lord's rejection or the latter days. The conqueror they were prepared for; the Sufferer—not knowing

---

* "His brethren, who had rejected him, forced by famine, are brought, by the path of repentance and humiliation, to own him at length in glory whom they had once rejected when connected with themselves. Benjamin, type of the power of the Lord upon earth among the Jews, is united to him who unknown had the power of the throne among the Gentiles; that is, Christ unites these two characteristics. But this brings all the brethren into connection with Joseph." (*Synopsis of the Books of the Bible.* i. 59.)

their own deep need—they have refused. Yet the
two are really one: even Benjamin was first Ben-
oni; and for them the Conqueror cannot be till
they receive the Sufferer; not the faith of a sufferer merely, but the One who has been this.
Power lies with Joseph, not with Benjamin.

But Joseph's heart longs after Benjamin: Christ
longs to display this character of power for them;
but for this they must be brought to repentance,
and He uses the ideal, prophetical Messiah to
bring their hearts back to Himself the true one.

Amid the sorrows of the last days this will be
accomplished for them. He who unknown is seeking them will make them realize their Benjamin as
Ben-oni, the son of sorrow, and that as the fruit of
their own sin (ch. xliv. 16). Benjamin is taken from
them: they have lost their part in Messiah as having rejected Him. All the depths of Judah's heart
are stirred; and in his agony for *Benjamin*, he is
met and overwhelmed by the revelation of *Joseph*.
They look upon Him whom they have pierced,
and mourn for Him as one mourneth for his only
son, and a fountain for sin and for uncleanness is
opened to them.

This, I believe, is the true, however meagre, interpretation of the type before us. But this brings
the whole nation into blessing under Christ; and
here, as far as they are concerned, the type (I suppose) ends. They are established in Goshen, and
the fat of the land of Egypt is theirs.

After this we read of the reduction of Egypt
itself under the immediate authority of the throne.
The people, bankrupt through the famine, receive
back their lands from the bounty of the king, returning him one fifth of the produce of the land as

the token of their indebtedness to the grace from which they have received all. Two tenths may remind us of the double claim of God upon us— by creation and by redemption. All the world shall own this in the day to come.

From chap. xlvii. 28, I think we have a separate part, an appendix to this history.

The Individual Application.—In the individual application certain broad features of Joseph's life are easy to be read, and these are all that I am able with confidence to speak of. It is plain how different in character is the suffering through which he passes to that of Jacob. Jacob's is disciplinary, the result, under God's government, of the evil of his own ways; Joseph, on the contrary, suffering for righteousness, the predestined path to glory: "if we suffer, we shall also reign with Him."

Child of old age is Joseph: how slowly, alas! the fruits of the new nature appear in us! Even for the saint, how true that "that which is first is natural, and afterward that which is spiritual"! Moreover, in the world through which we pass, all is hostile to the development of that which is of God. "He that separateth himself from evil maketh himself a prey;" and separation from evil is a fundamental principle of the divine nature. Hence persecution for righteousness, not only from the world, but even at the hands of those who, chosen out of the world, are still practicing conformity with its ways. Nay, one's brethren are, alas! often in this case *more* hostile than the very world itself, just because their consciences are more awake to a testimony which condemns themselves. And indeed how few are there among the children of

God who are thoroughly, and at all costs, subject to His Word! How many of all creeds, even the highest, whose code is liberty for self-will within certain wider or narrower limits! Thus, within the circle of professed Christian fellowship, how much real opposition which must be met by those who are Josephs, "adding," after the apostle's manner, disciples of the cross! Their path is individual, solitary often, save only for the God with whom they walk, and indeed because they have chosen to walk with Him. Yet it is thus a path of deepest, fullest blessing.

Rejected by his brethren, rejected by the world, Joseph carries with him the wisdom which interprets the scene around him, while master, too, of the circumstances by which he seems to be mastered. All things necessarily serve the One who is with him ever under all appearances, content Himself to find through seeming defeat His sure, eternal victory. Through all, he is preparing for the place where at last both his brethren are restored to him and also the world shall be his own: when Christ reigns, (of which we have been tracing the figures here,) His saints shall reign with Him.

Of this latter part, for the fullness of which we must wait to be with Him, we have nevertheless our anticipative foretastes. Even now, as the apostle tells us, the world is ours, long as it may be before we learn our spiritual supremacy over it. The word of life and of salvation is surely also ours as it was Joseph's, and it is ours to win to ourselves out of the world those who shall be in spiritual relationship to us also. This some would find as a type in Jacob's history, where it seems out of relation to the whole character and meaning of his life. It is Joseph rather, I believe, in whom we find this.

But while features of resemblance there necessarily are between the life of Christ as manifested thus in His people, and Him in whom alone it has been perfectly seen, yet the details, as remarked already, carry us continually away from the disciple to the Lord. This is surely designed and full of instruction for us. Is it not true that just so far as these features are developed in us it is the result of occupation with Christ Himself? "We all with open face beholding the glory of the Lord, are changed from glory to glory, even as by the Lord the Spirit." In preparation for the scene of His actual presence, He thus as we advance in spiritual life becomes the object upon which our gaze fastens. It is not we that live, but Christ liveth in us. He abides in our hearts by faith. We "grow in grace" as we grow "in the knowledge of our Lord Jesus Christ."

Thus, as the Nazarite's course ended, he came to the door of the tent of meeting to offer to God the various offerings in the value of which—not of his vows performed—he found acceptance with God; and there, thus standing, his hands were filled with the heave-shoulder of the ram, and the unleavened cakes of the meat-offering. Christ in the perfection of His blessed life, Christ alone upholding all things by the power of that in which in unique, matchless devotedness He glorified God, the Christ in whom we are accepted, fills, and for eternity is to fill and occupy, us only.

The subjective types of Genesis closing in the objective is thus not a defect, nor (I believe) a thought due to mere obscurity of vision as to what is presented here. It is to the "fathers" the apostle says, as characteristic of them, "Ye have known Him that is from the beginning."   And there he closes.   There Genesis closes too, with the vision of the glory of the Lord, suffering and exalted, the government laid upon His shoulder, the true Zaphnath-paaneah, revealer of the secrets of His Father's heart, Bridegroom of His Gentile Bride, Saviour of the world.   Where He fills the eye and occupies the heart, all else finds its just place and completest harmony ; communion with the Father is the portion of the soul, the power of the living Spirit realized.   And here what limit of attainment is imposed, save that which *we* may impose? The study of these Genesis-pictures will have done nothing for us, if it does not invite our hearts more than ever into the King's banqueting-house, where the everlasting arms inclose and uphold us, and "His banner" over us is "love."